Don't Get a
Make a Job

T0248449

*Inventive career models
for next-gen creatives*

Gem Barton

Laurence King

Published in Great Britain by

Laurence King Design
An imprint of Quercus Editions Ltd
Carmelite House
50 Victoria Embankment
London EC4Y 0DZ

An Hachette UK company

This book was designed and produced by
Laurence King Publishing Ltd, London.

A CIP catalogue record for this book is available
from the British Library

TPB ISBN 978-1-52942-036-4
EBOOK ISBN 978-1-52942-037-1

10 9 8 7 6 5 4 3 2 1

Book design: Turnbull Grey
Project editors: Gaynor Sermon, Felicity Maunder
Infographics: Russell Bell

Printed and bound in China by C&C Offset Printing Co., Ltd.

'Gen Z is entering the workforce on their own terms, demanding change with a new sense of boldness not seen in previous generations.'
Business Insider, February 2022

'Younger workers were hit hardest when the pandemic hit, entering an economy marked by a 14.7% unemployment rate, and 2021 grads had the hardest time finding a job last summer. But fast forward two years and one short-lived recession, and Gen Z is seizing the workforce in a way that shows they've already bounced back.'
Business Insider, February 2022

'Gen Z prioritizes different values at work ... 42% of Gen Zers would rather be at a company that gives them a sense of purpose than one that pays more, while more millennials (49%) and Gen X (56%) would rather work for a company that pays more.'

Business Insider, February 2022

Introduction

Much has changed since I had the idea for this book back in 2013. The first edition took nearly three years from pitch to shelf. This new edition took even longer, because each time I thought I had the new strategies all figured out, and found the perfect case studies to feature, things changed: new industries, new professions, new tech, new products, new forms of entertainment, new illnesses ...

The Covid-19 pandemic saw the world of work turned upside down in many predictable, and some less predictable, ways. There was working from home, agile working and remote learning, but we saw recruitment change too, from Zoom interviews to jobfishing, the employment scandal that saw dozens of creatives around the globe hoodwinked into working for a company that never existed.

But some things have not changed – the days of trading in your degree certificate for a nice safe job offer are (still) gone, and who knows if they will ever return? It is simply not enough to graduate anymore; the world demands more from you. You are the future, you are the next generation of entrepreneurs, design-thinkers, hyper-specialists and cultural agitators.

You have a role and you have a responsibility. It is no longer just about the world of design, it is about the design of your world!

You will be aware that the prospect of 'finding work' is tough. You will likely have heard nothing but horror stories since the economic downturn in 2008, followed by the impact of the global pandemic in 2020, yet you still chose a design degree, and you are still chasing that dream. Why? Because secretly, deep down, you know that the future will be led by free-thinking, forward-looking, rule-bending, problem-solving, question-asking social radicals, that's why! Think about the biggest problems we face today: poverty, dwindling energy resources and war. It is design, not money, that has the potential to solve these problems.

Our educated youth are ethical souls; they want to make a living, sure, but they also want to leave a legacy of betterment behind them for future generations, not just a collection of pretty things to be listed and honoured and drooled over in class. They are a powerful force, and one that doesn't plan on waiting for clients to commission them. They will be busy setting mousetraps of design excellence, subverting the balance of power away from those with the cash and towards those with the design ability. They are a hungry, motley, self-initiated crew, taking the world of work into their own hands. Gone are the days of 'getting a job' and welcomed is the age of 'making a life'.

Since 2008 and the global economic collapse, when banks virtually stopped lending, the majority of businesses and individuals became more risk averse as a result. This had an apocalyptic effect on the approach to securing work in the design industry. In such difficult times, as often happens, diamonds form from coal, and this very trying situation spawned a generation of fierce go-getters. Now that the floodgates have been opened, the design job market will never be the same again! No one can say for sure that it was the recession alone that inspired this shift, but if it had not been the recession it would have been something else, eventually. The natural instinct for change and progress will always be present in the creative industries. These early-Millennial-graduate-2008-recession-stalwarts now make up the majority of the workforce (many with hiring power). They experienced a time of uncertainty, and one hopes they are mindful of this when opportunities arise to work with the Gen Z creatives who were hugely impacted by the pandemic. If you are reading this, then that is probably you, and the fact that those 2008 recession stalwarts understand and respect your resilience should give you comfort, whether they end up being your colleagues or your competition.

There is a long history in the design world of trailblazers – the rare few who, for fear or fashion, feel the need to radicalize the process – but prior to 2008 the conventional route into practice was DEGREE>CV>FOLIO>INTERVIEW>JOB. This is a sensible equation that, if followed, would almost certainly get you a job, somewhere. There were always the few who had secured work experience in summer breaks, impressed people, kept in touch and been offered some work straight after graduation, but most of us simply followed the rules and hoped to goodness that we would be fruitful in the end. Many were indeed lucky, until the jobs dried up. It was then that the strong and the inventive found new ways to approach clients, to set up a practice, to specialize, diversify and subvert the traditions. While terrifying to be in the midst of, this is the time when new traditions are made, legends begin and the clock restarts.

By way of strategy-driven chapters, this book tells the stories of the new-generation trailblazers within our changing world. We explore their strategies, are introduced to their working methods and hear how and why they chose to make their own way. You will hear the stories behind the inception of designers and founders from all around the world.

You are advised against simply copying ideas from the bright sparks featured here. This book has been written with the intention of educating and inspiring you, to open your eyes to the myriad opportunities available. If there is only one piece of information you take away from reading this book, let it be this: if you cannot find an opportunity that you like or want, you owe it to yourself to make your own!

As a former student of architecture in the UK, now with 18 years of experience in teaching different design courses around the country, I have a unique insight into the world of both design practice and education. Having entered the architecture profession after graduating in 2006, I followed the 'traditional' DEGREE>CV>FOLIO>INTERVIEW>JOB route, securing a job in a medium-size practice. Less than eighteen months later, and just three months before my final accreditation exams, I received my first redundancy letter. As a relatively new graduate, I fell into the last-one-in, first-one-out trap. As with many of the case studies featured in this book, I knew that I had tough decisions to make, and I saw this negative as an opportunity to 'irritate the oyster', to make my own way and find – no, create – the perfect job for me. This took years and generated many tears along the way. I experienced a crisis of confidence brought about by fear of the unknown, so I stuck to what I knew, I rinsed my (then small) network of contacts and quite simply persevered. I had to take jobs I did not enjoy in order to make ends meet, and I dedicated all my free time to making work, meeting new people and developing my personal brand (what people say about you when you're not in the room).

I tried my hand at everything I could and then curated my working life based on my experiences. Today I spread my time between teaching, writing, designing and living. This recipe will not suit everyone, nor will it appear in the index of a careers manual, but for many like me, being in control of your destiny, being flexible, with the ability to spread risk, respond quickly and do something different every day is of the utmost importance.

One of my goals was to write a book to help others through some of the tough times I had experienced, and to reassure all those who don't fit the little job-shaped boxes that everything is going to be okay. In fact, it's going to be great. Boxes are for the ordinary, and who wants to be ordinary? The sooner I learned that not wanting the same things as everyone else made me unique, the sooner I realized I could become anything I wanted, even an author. What at one time I had perceived as my weakness ultimately became my greatest strength.

In researching the content and case studies for this book I scoured the globe for individuals taking their lives into their own hands. I have conducted interviews with every person in this book (and many more), as well as quizzing academics and leading industry professionals. I have rinsed my (now considerably larger) network of contacts and drained every single favour. With this new edition, there is also a greater focus on diversity of character, professions, voices and educational channels.

Don't Get a Job, <u>Make a Job</u>

Self-promotion

There was a time when expressing your strengths was considered egotistical or unsightly, or as 'showing off'. Many designers struggle with the idea of promoting themselves, but you need to make yourself visible in a competitive industry, right? Has social media changed all that?

Design firms receive an abundance of CVs and applications daily. So what can be done to make yours stand out? Most people put 'creative and hard-working' on their CV, but there is no better way to get that message across than to *show* an employer how creative and hard-working you really can be. Designers around the globe are becoming more and more imaginative in making themselves seen and heard, ensuring that potential employers and clients understand just how creative they are.

Your personal brand is powerful; it is what makes you who you are. In a tough market, the first hurdle is making sure that you are seen and remembered – for the 'right' reasons.

The Doubting Dog

Don't Get a Job, Make a Job

Strategy:

Don't be led by your audience

Catherine Unger

Since the start of Catherine Unger's career as an art director and 2D artist for computer games, she has worked on more than fifteen award-winning game titles, five of which received BAFTA nominations, and was both selected as a BAFTA Breakthrough (2020) and recognized as one of Apple's Ones to Watch (2021). It all began when Catherine and her sister drew comics as children, trying their best to make each other laugh. Now in her spare time she creates illustrations that she shares online with her 50,000 followers, and she continues to use social media as the primary way to promote herself.

Experience

My first experience of showing my art to others was between me and my sister when we were growing up. We would spend days drawing our own Dragon Ball Z comics for each other, trying to see who could make the other one laugh the most. I think this was a transformative time for both of us, as my sister also went on to make art for a living. It was my first taste of how having an audience can really drive creativity and push you to do better.

At university, where I studied illustration and animation, we used to have critiques at the end of each project where we would present our work to the whole class and our tutors. I didn't enjoy them one bit. I remember a room full of eyes and pensive faces staring back at me while I tried to convince them that what I had created was 'good'. It felt like a public execution. No matter how many times I did these critique sessions, they never became easier, and the anxiety leading up to them strangled my creativity. By the end of the course, I had fallen out of love with my own work, because I had moved so far away from my own processes in order

Tangle Tower

to appease a room full of other people. My work wasn't mine anymore.

During this period, the only place I felt more relaxed presenting my art was on websites like DeviantArt and Tumblr. In my head, it felt more private sharing work this way, although some people would argue that the internet is more public! The separation of the computer screen between me and my audience helped me compartmentalize the experience to be less personal, because I wasn't waiting for a live reaction.

I've heard people express how sharing work online can feel the exact opposite for them, that the thought of presenting art to the wider world can be terrifying. I try to visualize posting art like throwing a pebble off a cliff: once it's out there, it is out of my hands and all I can do is see how it lands. Just click the share button and detach. In most cases, the worst thing that can happen is that it doesn't receive many likes. Then I move on.

I think this is the reason why my preferred method of promoting myself is through social media. I will occasionally participate in networking

Character design for Tangle Tower

Designs for the mansion in Tangle Tower

> '*It's good to challenge yourself, but if you can find a method that works better for you, then follow your gut.*'
>
> Catherine Unger

events or presentations, but it's not how I make the best impression. Like many artists, I am socially anxious in real life. Promoting myself online helps me cheat my own insecurities and saves more room in my head to create art.

I rarely feel apologetic for deviating from more popular methods of being successful in this business, because I've found other ways to do things that feel less socially intimidating and could even reach a larger audience. Creating a video on YouTube could find audiences all over the world as opposed to doing a talk at a single event where only a certain number of people are in attendance. It's not better, it's just different. I always try to encourage people to find the way that keeps them enthusiastic. It's good to challenge yourself, but if you can find a method that works better for you, then follow your gut. There's no faster way to kill your drive than doing things you don't want to do all the time because you think you have to.

Advice

When I decided to take the leap to be a freelance game artist, I was leaving my first ever industry job and had no clue whether I would find work. We've all heard of freelancers experiencing droughts where they struggle to find work, and I wanted to avoid being in a situation where I couldn't pay my bills.

I took on more work than I had time for and settled for gigs that paid a lot less than I could afford. This scarcity mindset meant I ended up working at weekends and into the evenings on a regular basis, taking very few breaks. I had very high expectations of myself. This way of working wasn't sustainable. One day, I started to notice an ache in my drawing hand and it never really went away. Eventually, I was unable to draw.

I was recommended to a hand therapist and, after two years of recovery, I had to relearn how to do everything, from the way I pick up a kettle,

Above: Gibbon: Beyond the Trees
Left: Character design for Gibbon: Beyond the Trees

to the way I schedule my work week. Going through this experience showed me that the way I had been working wasn't viable long-term. Not just in a practical sense, like the way I was sitting or the equipment I was using, but the frame of mind and pressure I put on myself. It completely transformed the way I approach my professional life and I now have a healthier work/life balance. It's forced me to improve my ability to set expectations with clients, learn to say no, and encouraged me to increase my rates.

Strategy:

Put yourself out there

Skyler Fike

A proactive young man, Skyler Fike used the graphics skills he learned in architecture school and applied them to the production of a pamphlet as a unique tactic to 'sell himself'. His bold approach to networking and face-to-face meeting sets him apart from the inundation of faceless emails and printed folios that design studios receive daily. While this line of attack may not be appropriate for all employers and prospective employees, taking the time to research and identify his ideal work placement, coupled with his confidence to put himself out there, can clearly be seen to have been an effective method for Skyler.

Being mindful of your own goals and limitations is very important. Working for free for an unspecified length of time is not encouraged. Prearranging a time period and task list during which your suitability for the firm can be assessed could be an option. Skyler knew that during the economic recession he might have to do some work for free, but he set appropriate limitations based on his own financial status as well as his principles. Putting agreements in place before shaking hands on a deal ensures that everyone involved knows where they stand and prevents any confusion once the contract period is over. Don't be afraid of stating your intentions for a work placement, such as indicating any specific skills you would like to learn. This shows that you are a focused and dedicated young designer.

From being a 'Cheap Intern', Skyler is now a licensed architect with a practice in Texas and New York, and is building a new brand and reputation based on his interests in photography, acting and filmmaking.

Experience

My approach to the working world has not been a traditional one. After college I started by working for free at a local firm, which seemed to be the only viable option, given that unemployment was so high at the time. I had essentially given up on finding work when a mentor encouraged me to research architecture firms in the city, walk directly into the offices of those I liked, ask to speak to the partner and tell them I would work for free. While ethically I don't really agree with the idea of free work, it opened many doors that would not have otherwise opened for me, or at least opened so quickly.

As my method of execution, I researched firms and their partners and used fold-up pamphlets to display as much information as possible about my work, without being overwhelming. For each of the partners whose firms I walked into, I personalized every aspect of the process: casual firm, casual dress. At busy architects practices, I would stop by after 6pm, when things were shutting down (or just getting started!). I researched pictures of partners (if their website had them) and kept an eye out for architects I might possibly recognize at an event.

What happened next

I progressed into working for even more architects, but this time as a paid freelance worker. As I had hoped, the freelance position turned into a full-time job for a year and a half with another firm. By that time, two years later, I had either met, worked for or become closely acquainted with many of the major architects in the city.

Free can't sustain itself for more than a short time, so I only worked for free for about eight weeks. The Free Intern pamphlet turned into the Cheap Intern pamphlet and I began round two of walking into firms looking for part-time freelance work. Basically the same thing happened; I got 10 to 20 hours a week of work for each of the four or five architects that hired me. I worked freelance at

'Free can't sustain itself for more than a short time, so I only worked for free for about eight weeks. The Free Intern pamphlet turned into the Cheap Intern pamphlet.'

Skyler Fike

'Don't be afraid of stating your intentions for a work placement.'

Gem Barton

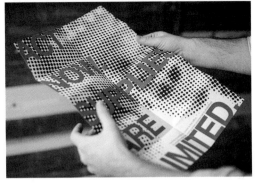

Free Intern pamphlet

offices and at home for about four months until I was hired full-time by an architect to whom I'd given a pamphlet four months prior but never heard back from.

One theme in my life has consistently held true: I was not meant for a desk job. I have learned that time and one's journey are non-renewable and that no one will protect those things except for me. After a recession and a global pandemic, I realize that nothing is guaranteed, and safety and security are an illusion.

Life is too short, so I chose to move to New York and use my experience as a photographer and architect to pursue my interests in film and acting. I can now look back over a decade of unapologetic self-protection, promotion and working for myself, and see how it led to where I am today.

The FYI
CONFIDENCE
and CV CLINIC

Monday 3rd June
5.30pm - 8.30pm

Hunter Collective,
EC1R 3AB

@findyourintern
findyourintern.com

Strategy:

Shoot your shot

Jasmine MacPhee

Coming from a small town in Cornwall in the UK, Jasmine MacPhee always wanted more than what she saw around her. The realities of a nine-to-five job and a samey routine were never going to work for her, so when she graduated in 2015 with a first-class degree in Fashion Promotion (specializing in graphic design), her aim was to turn her major project into a successful business. That is exactly what she did, launching the final iteration of Find Your Intern (FYI) in 2020. Starting as a platform on which to find paid-only creative roles, FYI grew into a flourishing community, online shop and live events – a key destination and tool for modern-day career advice and support.

'Show up, introduce yourself, prove you can do what they want.'

Jasmine MacPhee

Brand relaunch campaign slogan

Experience

I persistently practise what I preach, and I wouldn't be sitting here today without having self-promoted the hell out of myself professionally for the past seven-plus years. Without self-promotion, I wouldn't be working remotely while travelling to the world's most beautiful countries, making money from the things I know about, or building a successful commercial and personal brand.

Going for it, to get what I want or to help others, is in my DNA. I've always had a firm idea of what I want my life to look like, which makes setting my sights on something only I can obtain the only route. For example, my ambition when at university was to work for fashion editorials, and I knew I would need experience in the field before graduating. So I made a list of the top fashion magazines I wanted to work for and fired out my CV and folio (with no relevant experience). With that, I found success with *Cosmopolitan*, where I completed a two-week internship that paved the way for my next two editorial roles at *Marie Claire Runway* and *Harper's Bazaar*.

This approach, and my mantra 'shoot your shot', has brought me countless opportunities, including internships, permanent roles, freelance gigs and accelerating business ventures. If you don't show up, how will anyone get to know you? Show up, introduce yourself, prove you can do what they want. Before the launch of my business and throughout university, I promoted myself by going to events to forge industry connections that would help with the development of my business. I cold-emailed people that I knew would help with certain areas such as investment or app development. I needed to know this information in order to grow, so I took control and targeted the professionals who could help me. You have to get rid of the embarrassment of asking. It's a cliché because it's true, but if you don't ask, you don't get.

Fast forward to the relaunch of Find Your Intern in 2020, using Instagram as my main marketing tool. I self-promoted authentically, daily. Showing up on Stories as a personable, transparent face with whom my community connected and resonated led me to create a unique and successful brand. To be fully transparent, this daily social media self-promotion did lead to burnout, so you have to ensure it is manageable and doesn't drain your soul. Effort doesn't equal excellence.

Advice

Everything I have educated my creative community about is something I have been through myself. I have cried, failed and succeeded, and I am happy to bare all so that others can achieve. What makes me different is that I am not scared to be completely honest. I am fully transparent and that is why I have had huge success in creating a loyal and engaged community.

I have faced some turbulent personal adversity in my life and got to where I am now with serious hard work, a strong vision and determination. With an understanding of life and what people go through, alongside showing people 'How to Find a Job and Get Paid' I have offered them true understanding and support of their circumstances. Whether that's not having the family support or the financials, I want to show each and every young creative that they can find support and guidance when they need it. Opportunity can help you out of some dark places, and I only want them to flourish into their future, authentically.

Away from FYI, I am a Creative Educator and hold regular live events, workshops and virtual guest lectures to the top creative universities in the UK with one sole purpose: to empower and educate creatives on how to take the next step in their career and life journey.

Top: Initial concepts for FYI, 2015
Above: An FYI-hosted event

Don't be daunted by self-promotion

Advice on self-promotion from Alec Dudson, Founder and Editor, *Intern* magazine

Self-promotion is something that I long considered an undesirable necessity. For years, the idea of talking myself up in order to convince someone I was the bee's knees was one that I felt principled against. I wanted no part in these slippery and egotistical undertakings and figured that if people liked me and wanted to work with me, they would; if they didn't, they wouldn't.

Then I chanced upon an industry that I wanted to work in and my simplistic and clichéd perceptions had to evolve. Having studied sociology to master's level and decided that my tryst with academia had run its course, I was working full-time in the bars that I had worked in part-time during university. My amateurish exploration of photography as a means of creative output had stemmed from one of the units on my MA, and a post-graduation trip around the US left me with my first major body of work. I'd received some encouraging feedback about the photos and, when invited to start a website with some friends, effectively made my first step towards self-promotion in the creative sphere. That (now defunct) website went on to become a means of building my profile.

Initially, I mainly posted my own photographic output, but as the months passed I became interested in posting the work of others and interviewing them about it via email. My time away from the bar increasingly became consumed by the site, and having seen a couple of the others secure internships in the magazine industry using the website we had started as a reference, I built up the courage to give it a go. From having absolutely no background or agency in the creative sphere, in the space of eight months I had convinced the online editor at *Domus* that my self-taught 'editorial experience and knowledge of WordPress' rendered me a worthy extra pair of hands on campus.

I realized at that point I had proven my initial theory about self-promotion wrong. I hadn't done any sucking up, stabbed anyone in the back or lied – I'd simply taken the initiative and, in doing so, had real-world 'experience' that no one could deny me or invalidate.

The ability and confidence to be self-sufficient goes a long way to helping you stand out from the pack. The wider importance of that self-sufficiency is evidenced by the fact that 32 percent of creative workers in the UK are self-employed compared to just 16 percent of the overall economy, according to a 2021 report by the UK Government's Department of Digital, Culture, Media and Sport.

The cynics among you might simply call this 'blagging', but there is a difference, and that is substance. By being confident in what you have done and talking to others about it, you will find that those projects only gather momentum, until your next project better represents who you are and what you want to do. Talking passionately about your work will make people more inclined to collaborate with you, employ you and recommend you to others. I maintain that it is tremendously important to conduct yourself morally, being sure not to step on others to get ahead. Doing a job well is only one part of working in the creative industries; there are more people than ever out there who also have the skills to do the job. Your personality is your biggest weapon, and no matter how you dress it up (or down), as a creative, your personality becomes your brand as your reputation grows.

When I started *Intern* and got to the stage where finance was required, I turned to Kickstarter, a crowdfunding platform for creative projects. Research proved that as 'creator', I would have to inspire confidence in potential backers through as many means as possible. Effectively, when backing any crowdfunding project, an investor may be intrigued by the idea, but the creator is the person that delivers

it and, as such, it's them who the investor is taking a gamble on. From there on, I responded to every press enquiry I could, spoke at every event I could, and made sure that I thanked everyone who publicly backed the idea. My personal 'brand' was growing, and I've cultivated it carefully ever since. Nearly ten years in to that journey and I'm confident that I've not stepped on a single person to get to where I am. Treating my own self-promotion as an open-ended project, and taking opportunities to broaden my personal and professional networks, has allowed me to find new work in directions I'd never imagined.

In a post-pandemic world, where possible I'd encourage you to embrace opportunities to get out and meet other creatives, whether they're senior or junior to you, fellow freelancers or in-house. Being in control of your online self-promotion is a necessity, but deeper connections are forged far faster face to face. It may sound trite to say that the key to getting freelance work as a creative is about being in the right place at the right time, but it's true. You don't necessarily have to be selling and pitching, but starting conversations, finding shared interests and connecting with others on a human level will generate opportunities. If training yourself to be confident when talking about your work is proving difficult, just being yourself in creative social settings is a great way to switch gears and still ensure that people are finding out about you and the work you do.

Don't Get a Job, <u>Make a Job</u>

In motion

In the modern world, 'going mobile' means a number of different things pre- and post-pandemic. In the past, it has been a successful way of turning the tables on the conventional approach to winning work (such as entering competitions and bidding for commissions) and instead going public, hitting the streets, offering personability and flexibility. More recently, it also has a wider geographic interpretation, brought about by remote working, with the Zoom effect opening up possibilities previously out of reach because of time, space and logistics.

The following case studies introduce creatives who have used innovative methods of showcasing their skills and talents outside of the usual environments by taking themselves and their ideas away from the 'office'. Doing this increases your visibility and puts your work in front of people who may never otherwise have come across you and discovered how fantastic you are. Going public in this way offers flexibility and freedom, but it is certainly not easy!

Subverting the idea of the traditional approach is energetic and proactive, but it can also be difficult to sustain – can this approach work as a lone venture or does it need to be part of a greater master plan?

<u>Strategy:</u>

Go to the clients, don't make them come to you

icecream architecture

Having identified their goals early, the members of icecream architecture shrewdly took a separate academic course in business alongside their architecture studies. If you are thinking of setting up alone, then getting extra knowledge outside of your own discipline can be really valuable. Being able to balance your books as well as please clients and appease planners is extremely important.

If your business is consultation, then being able to visit and speak with the community is a top priority. icecream's van is essentially a mobile and highly approachable office – it is not so much about being big and beautiful (although that surely helps), but rather, more about accessibility and visibility. Choosing a fun, community-friendly icon such as an ice cream van – a vehicle we all have fond childhood memories of – was an astute decision. Having a hook that is a perfect match for your business needs as well as a strong brand identity is the ideal situation to put yourself in. Verging on performativity at times, the van, the activity, the display and exchange of knowledge and ideas attract attention, inquisition and footfall – the kind of attention large corporations pay marketing firms big bucks to achieve. On the following pages Sarah Frood explains how the company got itself on the road.

Fort William

Experience

icecream architecture was established in 2009 – after completing an intensive business-training course alongside our master's in architecture we stepped out and bought our van. The primary aim was not necessarily about getting noticed, but the van was a metaphor suggesting that, just like the ice cream van that enters communities providing a service on a daily basis, we would also take our services out to the community. At this point our drive was to approach architecture in a different way and, in doing so, also approach how we secured work and where we secured work. The exposed nature of the van instantly removed any barrier that might prevent people from approaching us. Though our experience was limited at this point we had a view on how most things should function both socially and economically. Our initial clients were looking for a more engaged method of practice, a way to better understand what the communities that they were working in needed or wanted.

'The exposed nature of the van instantly removed any barrier that might prevent people from approaching us.'

Sarah Frood

What happened next

The van quickly became a hook and a tool for engagement. It took us out of town halls and into the streets, and in a very practical way our ethos as a practice was personified by our brand and by the van. Its positioning during the work we undertook made the projects that we were working on more visible but also advertised icecream architecture to a new market, creating word-of-mouth growth to build on our initial contracts, and allowing our experience and the scale of work that we undertook to reach the required levels to enter the competitive tender market.

'Having a hook that is a perfect match for your business needs as well as a strong brand identity is the ideal situation to put yourself in.'

Gem Barton

Opposite top: Govan Book of Memories, Glasgow
Bottom: Public AA Strategy and Town Centre Chavette Denny, Falkirk
Below: Beyond the Fishing Line, Social Enterprise start-up incubator, Glasgow

<u>Strategy:</u>

Ideas can be generated anywhere

Vik Kaushal

Having studied architecture at university and with a first job as an art worker in youth and community groups, Vik Kaushal now runs Logan & Wilcox, a design studio for interaction, participation and production services in Manchester, UK. Vik plays at festivals, theatres and other cultural events all around the globe – a truly nomadic creative practice – as well as teaching architecture. With a strong sense of collaboration, Vik brings his determination and creativity into all his projects, utilizing his unique approach to design curated by dyslexia and making the most of opportunities presented to him in the wake of a fire in his studio.

Courteneers billboard

'All that my team needs to work is a laptop and an internet connection.'

Vik Kaushal

Experience

The prescribed routes that were presented to me seemed to fail me and didn't bear fruit. I was stunted in lots of ways because I was dyslexic and couldn't read and write very well. Being brought up in a traditional Indian family that ran a corner shop gave me an incredibly rich experience of meeting people from all walks of life. I think that experience gave me the confidence to speak to anyone on any occasion.

I originally went to the Glasgow School of Art to do my degree in architecture, and there I noticed that my favourite record label, Twisted Nerve, was doing a show down the road. As not many people are into psychedelic folk music, the show wasn't very well attended. In fact, there was only me and a few others there, including the label boss, Andy Votel. I approached him and struck up a conversation that lasted for over three hours and ended with him offering me work the next time I was in Manchester. I left Glasgow the week after to take up the role. Looking back, that conversation probably changed my whole life. The experiences and adventures I had during that period have been transformative and went a long way to increasing my expectations and ambitions for myself.

What happened next

In my practice, I don't have a regular studio space or a consistent office. I did for a while and it was fun. Having my own space, developing my practice and meeting other artists in the community was a productive time and I enjoyed it a lot. Unfortunately, after two years my studio was broken into and burnt down. This was devastating at the time, but it allowed me to cleanse myself of my old ways of working and pivot to a new direction. Thinking back, during the later period of my time in the studio I was mainly using the space to store stuff rather than to produce work. The new nature of the work required me to be agile and flexible, forming responses on the

fly to the situation at hand, and the artwork became more situated and site-specific.

All that my team needs to work is a laptop and an internet connection. Playing at festivals, it's common that we work from a bunk bed, on the train or in the car to and from the venue. I've even conducted meetings while sat in a field with 5,000 people watching a show.

The last few years have been transformative in the way that we work and communicate. We have seen almost a paradigm shift, with the world becoming accustomed to communicating via a screen. We saw our own work transition rapidly from physical, live, real-time performances to virtual events piped to your phone, laptop or Xbox. I personally found this an incredibly productive way of working. Meetings can be organized and held much more quickly, and any issues regarding a project can be ironed out collectively sooner. Additionally, being forced to work in this way allowed us to develop new modes and new mediums to work within and explore. I suppose the lesson is that ideas are not solely created in the office or the studio; ideas can be generated anywhere and everywhere, from a train trip with a colleague to the kitchen at a house party.

Above: Defected, 2022
Below: Hacienda 40th anniversary party, 2022

Strategy:
Bend the rules
Hank Buttita

For many, the need and desire to debunk the corporate, hierarchical job structure begins while still in education – feeling the grip of the institution can be an inspiration to challenge formalization, manipulate design briefs and stretch expectation. Enter Hank Buttita.

Preferring to make rather than draw, Hank charmed his tutor into allowing him to build his final design project rather than simply represent it through models and drawings. He invested US$3,000 of his own money – at any age this is a huge risk – showing the sheer passion and determination he had for his work. The completed project was picked up on inspiration websites across the globe. Hank believes that by bending the rules and being different he became noticeable, and being noticeable is a very useful commodity. Whether your desire is to get a job or to impress a client, the extended network that being a familiar name grants you is priceless.

Hank was entrepreneurial, keeping at the forefront his own designs for his future career, and with that he hit the road, en route catching the attention of the global press.

'Without stepping
outside the norm
to build my thesis
rather than draw
it, not only would I
have gone unnoticed,
I would have been
unnoticeable.'

Hank Buttita

Experience

In architecture school I was tired of drawing buildings that would never exist, for clients that were imaginary, with details I didn't fully understand. I prefer to work with my hands, exploring details thoroughly, and enjoy working/prototyping at full scale. So for my master's final project, rather than design a space that would never exist, I took a financial and academic risk by purchasing a used school bus for $3,000, and over the course of the semester I converted it into a tiny living space. I developed a presentation that focused not on the bus itself, but discussed the value of design through building and questioned the largely conceptual nature of architectural education.

Converting the space in less than four months was physically and mentally exhausting and nearly financially ruinous, but the risk and hard work paid off handsomely. The press generated by the project ultimately established my reputation and launched my career, connecting me with my first architectural clients.

After graduation, I teamed up with a friend who is a professional photographer to take the bus on a maiden voyage across the western United States. Through his fantastic photography we were able to spread the story of the bus and its conversion to people around the globe, expanding awareness of the tiny house movement and demonstrating the potential for small spaces to be both beautiful and functional.

What happened next

Over the course of seven years of architectural education, I came to realize that architecture is not the profession I imagined it to be. In order to stay engaged, I needed a certain level of hands-on interaction in design that doesn't currently exist. I wanted to prototype, and I wanted to build.

After graduation, instead of applying to firms I leased warehouse space and set up a small wood shop, centred around an old, beat-up 4x8 CNC machine. I have since been piecing together a freelance design career, tackling a variety of design and fabrication work to establish my business and stay afloat.

I was 'that guy' who spends all his time in the shop. Students looked to me for help with their models, structures and mechanics, professors hired me as a research assistant to develop solar ducts, and now I'm teaching a materials course at my alma mater, and my peers come to me for their digital fabrication needs.

Without stepping outside the norm to build my thesis rather than draw it, not only would I have gone unnoticed, I would have been unnoticeable. It's true that one of the most important parts of college is networking, especially in design. The goal of networking is to become a familiar name and get your foot in the door; even in the twenty-first century it is the most reliable way to find an employer or a client.

Now, with a unique, recognizable project to my name, my network has grown exponentially, connecting me with other professionals and potential clients all over the planet.

Hank Bought a Bus

The challenges of being a professional nomad

Advice on careers in motion from Melissa Sterry, design scientist, systems theorist and futurist

Not long ago, the direction of political, economic and cultural travel in many nations was towards building bridges, not borders. In Europe and beyond, though some world regions remained beholden to nationalism and protectionism, many embraced freedom of movement of goods, people and ideas. But, as the saying goes, 'all good things come to an end'.

Even before the geopolitical shifts of late, being a professional nomad was anything but straightforward, let alone as easy as many an Instagram account suggested. Whether your preferred work destination was a palm-fringed sandy beach or an architecturally sublime city, the world was your work-destination oyster. In practice, professional nomadism involves a lot of paperwork and, increasingly, a lot of hassle.

While you may think of yourself as a global citizen, overseas government agencies don't. From border control to tax offices, you are a foreigner. In the first instance, nomadism involves visa applications, which in turn typically involve providing evidence of having sufficient funds to afford your trip, proof of accommodation and information on who you are, what you do and what you plan to do. For longer stays you may have to provide evidence of your qualifications and other credentials. Having attained your visa/s, your next challenge is booking your various modes of transport. Again, this is simple in theory but no longer in reality as, in the post-pandemic world, many flight schedules are reduced. If you plan to drive on your travels, you'll need to navigate a system that sees the nations of the world subscribe to several different international licence schemes.

Unless you're a trust fund baby or have won the lottery, the biggest challenge you'll likely face when pursuing professional nomadism will relate to your finances, starting with your tax affairs. Every nation follows its own tax structures. Hence, even where a double-tax treaty exists, there's no rule of thumb. Making matters harder, even if you have the funds to afford a trans-border tax advisor, unless your assets are in seven digits you'll likely be hard-pushed to find one that's interested in providing you with the insight you need. As with issues of taxation more generally, the more diversified your folio of earnings (that is, the more side hustles), the more complicated navigating trans-border tax issues becomes. Added to that, whereas some nations, such as the UK, enable relative professional autonomy, others don't, meaning you shouldn't assume that your capacity to pursue your various career interests will be consistent from one nation to another.

Making things more complicated still, credit ratings agencies operate within national borders, meaning the moment an individual goes off (national) grid, their credit rating can go haywire, with the implications extending to everything from the interest rates paid on a loan to eligibility to rent or buy a home. And whereas those who are hired by overseas firms typically have their health insurance needs met, nomads will have to meet those needs themselves.

What steps can you take to mitigate these challenges?

• Do your homework. Don't assume how a nation runs its tax and other affairs. If you can't afford professional advisors, ask your peers for insights.
• Save, save, save. The moment you leave the place of your tax domicile you might start to lose the automatic right to some state services, such as healthcare. Don't rely on your projected income and instead build a reserve that can tide you over if the worst happens.

• Plan far ahead. Consider how your movements may affect your post-nomadic credit rating and what this may mean for your future plans.
• Safety first. Cater for all scenarios that may occur during your professional travels, such as medical emergencies and loss of income. Take out insurance policies and read the small print carefully.
• Put your support network in place before you go. Ensure that you have a community of supporters on speed dial on whom you can rely in every eventuality. Remember, everything from laws to cultural norms change from one nation to the next. Having friends, family and peers who can support you in a crisis can make all the difference.

Now for the good news … If you can overcome these challenges, taking your career on the road can deliver many dividends. Hands-on experience of working with other cultures provides invaluable and irreplaceable insights applicable to many fields. Working trans-border creates an understanding of how and why policies shape the destiny of nations and their citizens. While no panacea, nomadism can be an enjoyable and enriching experience, and provide opportunities to meet many extraordinary people you might otherwise not come to know.

Make a difference

With climate change, inequality, abuse of power, racism, misogyny, unemployment and poverty all around the globe, more and more people want to have a positive impact through the work that they do, not just make money, because there are many ways to judge value and success.

For many creatives, having a sense of purpose in what they are doing holds priority over higher salaries, but everyone deserves to be able to support themselves; it is possible both to do good and to make money. In this increasingly socially aware world, there can be stigma attached to earning money (a necessity for most of the population). You need to determine your own measure of value and recognize that monetizing those skills and talents is part of the journey.

The following case studies are examples of how making a difference can be about your past, present and future self, as much as about helping others.

SHUBZ at the V&A

Strategy:

Take a stand

Sound Advice

Inspired by 1990s rap labels, Sound Advice, co-founded by urbanists Joseph Zeal Henry and Pooja Agrawal, is a platform exploring spatial inequality. By mixing commentary and music, they debate provocative issues and advise on how to make change. They developed their enterprise more out of a sense of collective frustration than a need for the personal explorations of a creative practice. They felt that the architecture industry needed some disruption, to address its inequalities and give space to deal with the issues that mainstream architecture was avoiding – stories that were important but weren't being told or heard.

Since those early days, they have achieved incredible things, staying true to their ethical framework and mission to create a place on the periphery, allowing for care, pluralism and equity to be foregrounded and holding an uncomfortable mirror up to the architecture profession through publications, events and multimedia creations. Joseph Zeal Henry outlines their vision and practice on the next pages.

We Are Here at the Rio, Dalston

Experience

Conceived more as a platform than a practice, Sound Advice was set up to explore 'spatial inequality in architecture through music'. More recently, it has become a creative agency 'exploring new forms of spatial practice through music'. The writer Toni Morrison spoke about how musical culture is foundational to Black creativity, and this was a good starting point from which Sound Advice could build. As a practice, we have a tense relationship with certainty that developed out of improvisation, circumstance and the need to continuously update and shift the focus and interest as we produce more work and projects.

Built from the ground up, and utilizing networks of people rather than relying on patronage from existing institutions, 1990s rap record labels were a blueprint for Sound Advice. Much like labels such as Roc-A-Fella, Bad Boy and Cash Money, we wanted to tell our own authentic stories in our own voice. It takes time, but you should feel confident that you can create something that people will engage with.

A good example was our event SHUBZ at the V&A for the London Design Festival. We wanted to celebrate the cultural significance of the Shubz, a predominantly London phenomenon usually hosted in domestic spaces or small local social infrastructures to create a more informal night and dance culture. The concept of the Shubz was – and still is – a space for communities who struggled to be represented culturally or even allowed into formal nightclubs. The video installation by Sound Advice showed some of the groundbreaking music videos that captured the domestic landscape of the global diaspora in Britain. Obviously, not everyone was aware of what Shubz meant – someone asked me what time 'Shubz was arriving' – but it created a moment to share our culture.

Our book *Now You Know* gathered the thoughts and reflections of more than fifty architects and urbanists of colour to address the discrimination baked into our built environment. No one had previously developed a project like this, and it was unlikely that anyone else would have. An enterprise had to be created to publish such a project.

Our collaborators are always people who understand a different medium better than we do, whether that is using a professional graphic designer or commissioning incredible photographers to capture our events. It is important to understand where your limits of practice are and to work with others to fill in those gaps. We are particularly interested in the stories that people want to tell, and we spend time as a practice to understand these perspectives and build collaborations from there.

It is important for us to keep an open mind on what is relevant to our central form of creative practice and to stay away from the trap of being purely self-referential within our own creative discipline. It is also important to take risks and to be brave. That creates the space to find new modes and methods to produce projects and work.

Advice

Try to find space that allows you to practise in a way that is authentic to you and your interests, rather than trying to create something that mirrors and tries to emulate something else within your practice. Try to make the starting point something outside of your world. You have to find value in the practice and the work in its own right.

It is important to take time to develop a critical position and shape the narrative around your practice – don't rush that process. We took time before deciding to work on large and complex projects. When we were interviewing the American architect Teddy Cruz for our residency at the Centre for Canadian Architecture, he made a point that resonated with us, which was that he had to 'build a position before building buildings'.

'Try to find space that allows you to practise in a way that is authentic to you and your interests.'

Joseph Zeal Henry

Strategy:

Bet on yourself

Stacie Woolsey

A true innovator, Stacie Woolsey is reinventing art education. Dissatisfied with the broken system of post-graduate education, Stacie decided she wasn't willing to miss out on the master's experience simply because she was priced out of the market – so she created her own programme. She reached out to four practising designers that she admired – Thomas Thwaites, Alexandra Daisy Ginsberg, Seetal Solanki and Marie Tricaud at Room Y – and asked each of them to set her design briefs to complete in her own time. Over 18 months, she completed all four projects and then held her own degree show titled 'Make Your Own Masters'. Now she helps others do the same! In 2020, 11 'students' who faced barriers to learning, whether due to finance, ethnicity, age, location or disability, took part in the pilot cohort.

MYOM x Makerversity

Experience

I was never a commercial designer. I was creative, but I never knew exactly what I was or what I wanted to do – I still don't. I left university with a BA in Graphic Design, and I certainly was not a graphic designer. I did the interning rounds, and I spent part of my time working in start-ups and ad agencies and ice cream vans. I didn't have a clue what I was doing, but I had done my research and knew exactly where I wanted to end up. Interning in London is far from easy. I was trying to pay London rent on a small wage, with work that was only guaranteed for three months at a time, propping myself up with bar jobs and any scrap of work I could find, and just trying to get my foot in the door in an industry that relies heavily on 'who you know'. I needed to take control of this thing for myself, and that's when the idea to do an MA started.

Lack of access to postgrad education is something everyone just accepts, but why in 2023 are we still having conversations around education in the UK being a privilege, and ultimately elitist? This isn't just for people who want to do an MA, it's for those who want the opportunity to reach the top of their field and develop a practice that takes them there. I learned the hard way, but all the hard work in the world doesn't mean success; there are a lot of barriers in the way, especially within the creative industry. The luxury of an MA is the time to develop and understand what you actually do as a creative. A BA education is accessible to most people in the UK, albeit by accruing tens of thousands of pounds of debt, but MA programmes are not built the same: if you can't afford the fees, you can't go. Yet beyond financial barriers, education, institutions and industry are not inclusive places, and alternative pathways need to be built to access them. Many leave education, experience huge knocks in confidence and really lose their way, and it's not their fault: the system is just not set up to work for a lot of people.

Dirty Soaps

Building my own education programme was an experiment. I never knew whether it would work, and many times I felt that it wasn't working. There was a period towards the end when I had almost completed my projects and I decided to name my customized MA and practice. I came up with the title 'Anthropological Futures'. Putting real words and meaning to all the work and learning that I had done and had been doing throughout my education was a moment that hit pretty hard. All I could think was, 'oh my god, this thing actually worked', and it worked better than I could ever have anticipated.

What happened next

Make Your Own Masters has become a project bigger than me as an individual. The response from press, brands, industry and institutions has been overwhelming. Yet the most important response has been from people just like me, those stuck with a lack of options on what to do and where to go next.

I hope the legacy of this project proves to people that if you find you can't do something for whatever reason, you've stumbled upon an opportunity. You call yourself a creative or a designer, and you design and create yourself a solution. There are more people than just you that have wound up there.

It's not easy, but I can't express enough how worthwhile it is taking a gamble on yourself and trusting in your abilities until everyone else does. Unless you are incredibly lucky you don't just get handed opportunities: you have to make them for yourself.

Top: MYOM 2021 Showcase at Somerset House, London
Above: 2021 alumni Liim Studio

'I found myself priced out of education, so I decided if I can't buy an MA how do I make one?'

Stacie Woolsey

eeH debut clothing campaign, 2021

Don't Get a Job, <u>Make a Job</u>

Strategy:

Be the change you want to see

Estelle Ebenga Hénot

Estelle Ebenga Hénot spent years following the traditional path, which made her feel trapped. But now every day and every project is different, and she feels more alive. That is because she would not accept the status quo. She knew change was needed and she took full control and immersed herself in that challenge. Her first creative design job was as artistic director for a festival in Lille in 2011, and she created her own association, Ladies of the Ground, to promote women in hip-hop. Today she runs eeH, her own creative agency and content production company, consulting on diversity and inclusion topics for brands in the fashion and lifestyle sectors.

Experience

When I quit my job as a digital content manager in 2018, I promised myself I would create more opportunities for Black and Afro-descendant people in creative industries. I used to work in the jewellery industry, which is not the most diverse world, and I know what it is to be the only person of colour on a team, or to struggle to find an internship or your first job in the fashion, music or advertising industries. This shouldn't be the case today, especially in a city like Paris, but unfortunately the French mentality is different than in Anglo-Saxon countries.

I started as a freelancer, chasing clients and working on various projects in different industries without having a real purpose, but then I realized that I had to find my own purpose so as to not suffer from my work. I grew up with hip-hop culture, which is one of the most widely consumed cultures in the world, and I understood that brands needed to integrate its insights into their campaign strategies, but they didn't have the tools or the people in their teams to make it happen. I am part of this culture, and I embrace it daily, so I understood I had something to bring.

I started my podcast Inside the Cypher to gain more insights from people from our culture. This is how I shaped my profile as a culture specialist. People already knew me as a dancer, or as a blogger with my previous website Groovy Brain, but my podcast was something else because it was full of interesting insights. Then I started to reach out to brands to get new freelance opportunities and introduce my skills as a specialist.

One of my big projects has been to create a women's contemporary streetwear brand, and that led to teaching Entrepreneurship in a fashion business school in Paris. When I was looking to recruit, some of my students were struggling to find an internship to validate their year, most of them Black girls. It reminded me of what I went through during my student years. I took three of them into my company as interns because they couldn't find positions elsewhere. They had been looking for internships for months, and I just had to offer them an opportunity.

What happened next

I wish I had found someone like me to help me keep believing during my studies, because it's easy to give up or just to find bread-and-butter work that is intended to be temporary, and instead get trapped in that routine.

We need more representation to show that it is possible to make our dreams happen, to believe in the career we want to have, and to let other girls have these opportunities, especially in the fashion and lifestyle industries: it's a trend to feature Black people on mood boards but they also need a seat at the table and to be on company boards. If I can make it on my small level, I do it.

'When I say "my work" I mean the job I've built, that made me build myself.'

Estelle Ebenga Hénot

Estelle hosting her podcast Inside the Cypher at
The Notorious IBE Festival, Heerlen, in 2022

Know that you can

Advice on making a difference from Sara Vaughan, Innovator, Creator of Global Brands with Purpose, Positive Change Maker and Host of the Start Somewhere Podcast

I made my current job. Or rather I should say jobs, for I am a purpose polymath. I would love to be able to say that this was due to some amazing plan and great foresight on my part. The truth is, it absolutely, wasn't!

In fact, it took me a while to start somewhere on my purpose journey. Working on the launch of Forevermark, the ethical diamond brand, was the turning point in my life, when I realized I wanted to create powerful brands and movements for positive change that addressed and solved the world's most pressing issues. That led to a role at The Body Shop, where I was responsible for their global brand repositioning – Beauty with Heart and The Stop Sex Trafficking of Children and Young People Campaign. This was the largest corporate-led petition ever presented to the United Nations, generating some 7 million signatures and effecting change in trafficking legislation in more than twenty countries. I then went to Unilever, where I looked after Sustainable Business for all the categories and brands and created the All People Are Beautiful brand for Unilever Personal Care. I also worked on the brand purpose for the 16 biggest Unilever brands, including Dove, whose Self-Esteem Project will have reached some quarter of a billion young people worldwide through their educational programmes by 2030.

I then became the Global Chief Purpose & Sustainability Advisor to *Marie Claire*, which reaches 91 million women and girls around the world, giving readers ideas and inspiration for making long-lasting, impactful positive environmental and social changes through the articles I wrote and also through the creation of the game-changing *Marie Claire* Sustainability Awards and *Marie Claire* Sustainability Festival.

Today, I have my own consultancy working with leading companies and brands to innovate, create and develop, and implement their purpose and timebound deliverables to tackle pertinent social and environmental issues. Additionally, partnering with some incredible visionaries, I create and/or catalyze positive global movements for change – such as helping to stop the tide of single-use plastic with A Plastic Planet or changing the fashion industry as a Fashion Avenger with Project Everyone.

So how best to get started if you want to make a difference in the world? Here are my top tips:

1. First off, *know that you can.* For you are very powerful. A better world is not just a pipe dream. It is something that we can create together. As we have seen, small collective actions can become very powerful global movements. As Greta herself has proved, 'No One Is Too Small to Make a Difference'.

2. If you haven't already, *find your own purpose.* Your why. The cause that matters to you. Whatever that may be. Each one of us is unique. Thankfully so. Honour it and live by it. As Kate Robertson, Founder of One Young World and co-author of *How to Make a Difference* says, 'Real change is made by ordinary folk trying to improve the world one person and one change at a time'.

3. *Take action now.* As David Attenborough says in *Seven Worlds, One Planet*, 'We can improve things if we determine to do so. This is a crucial moment. The decisions we take now influence the future of animals, humanity and indeed all life on Earth.'

4. Exercise the *purpose that is in your pocket.* As Anna Lappé, the writer and activist, reminds us, 'Every time you spend money you're casting a vote for the kind of world you want'.

5. *Embed purpose* into your start-up/business/brand, whatever its size. Act on it and tie it to your commercial success. Make your case to your boss if you have one. Being purpose-led isn't just a nice to do. It's an essential to do. For in this fast-changing VUCA (volatile, uncertain, complex and ambiguous) world of ours, it is only genuinely purpose-led companies and brands that will survive.

6. *Think big.* Get yourself some great work experience and mentors to help you navigate your journey (have a listen to my podcast for some ideas on who they might be). Be brave and shoot for the stars. Reach out on LinkedIn, Twitter or whichever platform they are on. I promise you, even if they say no, they'll be flattered to be asked. So go for it!

7. *And finally … Enjoy it.* Helping people and the planet is good for them and good for you. Do it and not only will we have a healthier world, we will also have a happier one. For in doing so, you will find more energy, more excitement and more joy than anything else in life.

Don't Get a Job, <u>Make a Job</u>

Specialism and diversity

Having a specialism, being unique and putting all your eggs in a perfectly designed basket can be scary. However, as the world diversifies and our needs and wants vary, it becomes increasingly important to be able to offer something different. Pursuing your interests is always a good bet – if you like what you do, you're likely to do it well. The following specialist case studies have carved niche markets from a hectic design landscape. If you do something very specific and you do it well, you can quickly and easily become the go-to person for that task. Get focused. Be special.

The rise in diversification (or generalism, as some call it) has been paramount in the last 20 years, and to stay afloat many companies and individuals have 'covered their bases' by providing more than one service and spreading risk. In times of economic uncertainty this is a valid business move; however, there are a number of driven individuals for whom this creative balance is just their way of life. The following diversifiers and specialists have used the wide range of skills learned in their design courses at university and applied them to a vast set of actionable projects.

Mall-terations

Don't Get a Job, <u>Make a Job</u>

Strategy:

Learn from your idols

Stereotank

The route into specialism can be intentional – addressing a niche not catered for in the market – or accidental, following your instincts and desires and discovering naturally recurring themes.

Both of these were the case for architecture and design duo Marcelo Ertorteguy and Sara Valente, aka Stereotank. With independence being the ultimate goal, prior to forming Stereotank the pair separately sought out experience in similarly situated practices in order to learn the necessities of operating as a business within their chosen field. This is a smart move. Exposing yourself to the types of situations you are likely to encounter while being mentored by others is an excellent way to prepare for the eventualities of conducting business independently. It should not be looked upon as 'spying', but as research, training and groundwork. This also prepares you for the future, as one day these may be the same firms you will compete against for projects and clients.

Experience

We didn't deliberately choose specialism over diversification, it just happened naturally by starting to work with our favourite subjects. Objects, themes and ideas started to recur, creating a body of work with a defined direction and a vision. This portfolio is what has made everything happen. Each one of the projects gave a hint to make possible the next; there is no better publicist than your own built work.

As designers and artists we are mostly attracted to the non-conventional; we like to reinvent the wheel over and over again. Going back to basics always offers an opportunity for new insights, ways of looking at old things anew, with a fresh eye.

Being independent is the ultimate desire. Even though schools work as a laboratory for the professional practice, they never give you the real sense of exposure needed to be independent. Investing the first few years out of school in a practice with similar interests to yours could be very beneficial for your professional career; in order to 'kill your idols' you must know them well.

Collaborations are essential for professional growth; usually they are productive when team

Cyclo-Phone

members complement each other, when each member offers what the others lack. Collaborations are also very positive when members with similar mindsets participate, having a healthy and productive competition.

In our case, a collaboration was the opportunity to make our first project happen in New York. It was a collaboration on multiple levels. We teamed up with two other designers (combo colab) and together applied for a grant offered by the Department of Transportation of New York through a non-profit organization (Hester Street Collaborative) that presented our proposal, which became known as 'Mall-terations'. The installation, built in 2009 and in place for over two years, celebrated the history of immigration on the Lower East Side neighbourhood by portraying historic facts painted on the floor in parallel with railroad track graphics that evoked the old elevated tracks, while five colourful benches that rotated 360 degrees enlivened the park.

In New York the majority of the job opportunities for architects are in high-end residential, commercial, boutique design, hospitality and some infrastructure; few small studios are able to focus their practice on projects where art and creativity are at the base of the endeavours, making the opportunities to work in this field very limited. This was one of the reasons why we found ourselves in the position of creating our own niche in the design world.

Having gone down the traditional route for some time prior to finding our own path taught us two important lessons; on the one hand it gave us the opportunity to see the profession from a standpoint that we couldn't have had as recent graduates on our own, and on the other hand it made us demand more from ourselves, creating a greater necessity for independence. The more freedom you have, the better you can think, and the better you can think, the happier you are.

Little Free Library

'Specialization can be as broad as diversification; by choosing one path you "limit" yourself to a whole set of possibilities.'

Stereotank

Stereotank House

What happened next

After our first ten years in New York working with established architectural practices while creating our own studio in parallel, we were offered a position to teach at the School of Architecture at Florida International University in Miami. We decided to move, as the idea of teaching had always been exciting to us, and also because working at the school would open up more time and offer the flexibility to keep developing our practice while expanding our research and our network.

Five years have passed since we relocated to Miami. Admittedly, too many changes at once are certainly overwhelming – new context, new job, family growing, new projects – but all this has enhanced our survival skills to adapt and grow stronger and more resilient.

In Miami, we decided to invest our savings in developing a project that would be our proof of concept, marketing tool, home and studio, all at the same time. We bought a 5,000-square-foot vacant lot and designed and built a 700-square-foot house prototype, reusing shipping containers as the main structure. While shipping containers might not sound like the most fitting construction type for Florida's very hot and humid weather, we embraced this as a challenge to 'tropicalize' the shipping container by integrating it with shading devices and reflective surfaces to keep the building cool (in both senses of the word).

The Woodlands Wind-O

Through this project we have been able to meet great clients with similar interests to ours, as well as creating a network within the building and design industry in this city that is new for us. We are currently designing a 'Micro Campus' for a creative couple who teach filmmaking to underserved communities and a house for a couple of biologists and environmentalists with specific focus on sea level rise and sustainability.

Besides stepping into bigger projects and undergoing the growing pains these entail, we also keep working on small public art projects. In 2018 we won a competition to design a bench at the Woodlands, Texas. For this project, we wanted to create a street furniture piece that would engage the users and the landscape simultaneously, while keeping a sculptural character. In 2021 we were commissioned to design a 'place-making' device for the Story Teller Garden in Allapattah's Public Library. For this opportunity, we came up with the 'Sound Cactus', a public art installation that invites users to listen and share stories, news, audiobooks, radio and music.

'It should not be looked upon as "spying", but as research, training and groundwork.'

Gem Barton

Sound Cactus

Measures: Weight

Strategy:

Repeat, repeat, improve, repeat

Fabrice Le Nezet

Sometimes you just know! Designer and maker Fabrice Le Nezet knew that he would never be 100 percent satisfied by a traditional job and, rather than fighting that realization, he embraced it – he decided to get a freelance job that would feed him and also give him enough free time to focus on his own work.

Through years of refinement and design iteration, Fabrice established his own unique style. Having a trademark style can be seen as a drawback to some, suggesting that you are not able to fully let go of the design process and hand over to a client's wants. Fabrice disagrees, believing that, by developing a style that is instantly recognizable as you, *you* become instantly recognizable – well, we can all spot a Wes Anderson film from 1,000 paces, can't we? When you are not afraid of doing the same things over and over, you are free to improve and develop. This iterative process is inherent in the world of design. Repetition can be a positive measure; Fabrice calls it his quest to extract the essence of his work.

'Being specialized doesn't mean doing the same thing forever.'

Fabrice Le Nezet

Fashion for Concrete

Experience

I have been working within a director collective for a few years now, producing very diverse work, from short films to music videos and TV commercials. We always try to explore different styles and push for every project to be a new experience. Our work has generally been very well received but sometimes we notice people struggle to picture our style easily and to recognize our work. When I started working on my own, I had no other goal than producing what I had in mind. However, project after project, I discover my approach to the creative process has completely changed.

Being specialized is a key point for me. By 'specialized', I mean developing a unique style, something that everyone can recognize in my work. Every project you take on will advertise your work and your artist profile as a whole and create connections in people's minds. This way, you might potentially have people directly contacting you because they like what you do. The recurrent use of painted metal tubes and concrete volumes in my sculptural work is a trademark for me. Even though the concepts behind the projects differ, the works can be easily linked.

By talking with other designers, I have discovered that many artists are doing far more diverse projects than you would expect. Generally they won't communicate about those projects, not because they don't like them but because they don't fit their image. So even if I want or have to do very diverse things, I think it is important to ostensibly keep a clear profile.

What happened next

After a couple of years developing various artistic projects and freelancing on the side, I felt tired of constantly running after time to develop my own projects. The balance was off and I thought I should find a way to spend more time on my own practice. I was introduced to still-life photographer Dan Tobin Smith when he was looking for someone to help him develop a new creative studio, Optical Arts, focused on creating experimental work at the intersection of photography, animation and film.

I now feel very lucky to work in a creative environment where I can keep developing my own voice and where quality is pretty much the only thing that matters. In this job, I finally have the opportunity to combine everything I love, from architecture to sculpture to experimental filmmaking.

I joined Optical Arts in 2019, so I was there for the duration of the pandemic. Because our team is quite small, we were able to regularly meet each other in the office while maintaining social distancing. It was a great social support in those times when we couldn't go out much.

The development of remote work combined with Brexit (in the UK) and the increase in demand in the animation industry had quite an impact on us. In the last two years, it has become harder to find good artists to work with. The nature of the work we do is quite specific, therefore training is at the centre of my work at Optical Arts. While working remotely with experienced freelancers has been pretty smooth and efficient, I have found it harder to help and transmit knowledge to younger team members when they are not in the same office.

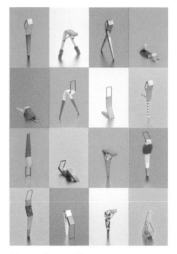

Above: Spring/Summer 2012
Below: Utopia

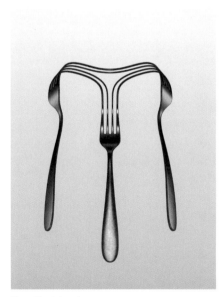

Top: Phototrophs
Above: Fork

Advice

It is useful to develop strong technical skills alongside your artistic research – that way you will be able to easily find your first job. This might not be your dream job, but it will give you the financial independence to carry on your research. Paradoxically, the ideal job is the one that does not quite suit you 100 percent. Indeed, I would say ideas often come from frustration. Generally, I get loads of new project ideas when I am stuck on some really boring job. Obviously finding the right balance isn't easy and is something you have to question all the time. That said, I also think being able to adapt to different mediums is important. This can be an interesting way to renew and open your perspective.

Specializing doesn't mean having to do the same thing forever. You might get bored of it at some point or, even worse, you might get bored of your own work. Step by step, you can drive

Stills from The Cliff

your style in new directions and, if you want to try something new, go ahead; with time you will find the connection. I started working on some toys, which developed into more minimalist and sculptural concrete toys, which finally ended up as actual concrete and metal sculptures.

'By developing a style that is instantly recognizable as you, *you* become instantly recognizable.'

Gem Barton

Futurofono

Strategy:

See doubt as a tool, not a weapon

Jocelyn Ibarra

Jocelyn Ibarra is founder and showrunner at the Time Travel Agency. This is a very different kind of design company, one focused on the questions of tomorrow, rather than the problems or solutions of today. The agency operates under the cover of a speculative design studio in the Nordics, Canada, Italy, the United States and online, and specializes in combining immersion, world-imagining, deep games, prototyping and the collaborative Web3. By making tools and experimental experiences (such as Speculative Day of the Dead and the Laboratory of Donated Dreams), they help people reach their futures in order to imagine them differently.

'Surround yourself with people who want your success.'
Jocelyn Ibarra

Experience

Working for myself offered me the most control over intellectual and creative processes, which was denied to me everywhere else I tried. I avoided traditional methods because I couldn't find agency over my present and future in the promise offered to the generation before me. What I sensed as realistic, possible, and ultimately worthy was to make my own path. Lately, I have been reflecting on the role that certainty, uncertainty and doubt played in my story and in the decisions I made. To me, 'tradition' is based on what seems like a false certainty. So I embraced uncertainty. I doubted. Over the years, I became comfortable with doubting and with being unsure, and, most importantly, with using this to my advantage. I found balance and resilience in doubt; I saw doubt as a tool, not a weapon. As such, the formulation of the Time Travel Agency was rather unplanned. We had been happily working in our corner, following a process that was a living organism adapting to the situation in front of it, when someone suggested using the book *Speculative Everything* to frame our work. From our point of view, we had just been passionate and relentless about our interests for years, always after different themes and outcomes, and adaptation had been the surest method of survival.

We refuse to be derailed by the argument that fantastic futures are not useful. Being an artistic studio at heart, we use art's transformative envisioning to deliver dreams, and we continue by landing them in 'real life' next. The only non-mystery at the Time Travel Agency is that we use art to express futures simply because that's how we can express ourselves better.

Somehow, aiming to be unique has brought a lot of freedom. I believe this freedom provides artists and creatives who want to make it on their own the space to focus on their process – the core of uniqueness. Having a specialization means that we became good at surviving, so we decided to put that at the core of our offering and teach our clients how they could do it too. Working in the futures field is just a gorgeous excuse.

Our process is full of mysteries and unknowns. We work with immersion, fiction and ritual; meaningful play and symbolic enactment allow us to explore deep themes. We spend a lot of time on prototypes because they help our minds to prioritize, and because they engage our clients with our process and its 'safe chaos'. One of our clients described working with us as a unique process that taught them how to be better at their job by taking a trip inside themselves to find answers, as opposed to getting better solely by using trends and signals from foresight and futures thinking, disciplines that deal with what is 'out there' and what is already here.

Experiences like Speculative Day of the Dead, the Laboratory of Donated Dreams and Futurofono are just the manifestation of a realizable idea – it's the shine, the dreamspace that our clients

Above and below: Speculative Day of the Dead

Palindrome

Don't Get a Job, <u>Make a Job</u>

imagined and we produced. At their heart, they are strategies to follow to make the shiny graspable, relatable and real.

Because we follow a niche strategy, we have been able to expand on the uniqueness of our process, and design tools that sustain its every stage. Palindrome, depending on the order in which you use it, is a speculative design toolkit or a game of futures, and its order/use depends on what our clients need. It is the tool we use in our consulting practice so our clients see their own future before they exist in it in later months. It is a tool of agency, and the first stage when working with us. It supports the idea that if someone does not have agency in their future, it will be too difficult to know what to do with a preferred future.

The Laboratory of Donated Dreams

Advice

Take your individual art form and move people with it. Surround yourself with people who want your success. If you go into this adventure knowing that there will be struggles on any path, let me assure you that this struggle is worth it. Be kind to others; prioritize hiring underprivileged individuals; be proud of the person keeping it all together; protect your values; say no and move on; and don't take any bullshit.

'Having a specialization means that we become good at surviving.'
Jocelyn Ibarra

Little Towers

Strategy:

Embrace the 'busyness'

Adam Nathaniel Furman

Some people are born to juggle – they are at their happiest, most switched on and inspired when multiple activities and connections are possible. Adam poetically refers to their multiple interests (architecture, design, making and writing) as their 'children', each running around independently, yet intrinsically connected. They say that they have no favourites and all make up the dynamic of the family as a whole. Their particular approach to authenticity and aesthetic is captivating. With expanding markets and ideas, Adam doesn't just take care of a creative household, they take care of an entire village.

Working in many areas is not always an efficient mode of practice; each takes time to nurture and master. Diversifiers are likely to find they spend much of their free time busying themselves with side projects and learning new techniques, but the possibilities these endeavours create are infinite.

Just like Adam, diversifiers have to be agile, nimble, proactive go-getters – they want it, they need it, and they make it happen! The ferocious appetite for success and the ability to curate such a lifestyle are traits no client or potential employer can ignore.

'I did all my work in the evenings, early mornings and weekends; the quintessential geek on their own at the computer is just my way of working.'

Adam Nathaniel Furman

Experience

I have found that I enjoy working on several things at the same time, and I find it difficult being without any one of them. It's a little like having a big family with lots of kids running around the place, juggling all their needs, and it being a bit hectic at times, but the household being full of love and joy because of it. So journalism, poetry, film, product design, art, interiors, architecture and ceramics are all like the kids that I want to spend an equal amount of time with, and who play with each other, teaching each other the things that they learn and bring to the family individually.

It was virtually impossible for me to break into the world of design and media and publicity through a normal route – my stuff doesn't fit in well enough – so the internet was vital. I could put my own work out there without the need for approval from any gatekeepers, and people found it and gave me the sense that it was worthwhile to carry on. Initially on blogs, then on Tumblr, then Twitter and Instagram, I found my own little audience, which eventually grew wider, and while it is still relatively niche, it eventually caught the attention of progressive corners of mainstream media. The internet allowed me to do weird, complex, difficult work that still found an audience, without the need to dumb anything down for any generic 'market segment'.

For the first seven years or so after graduating I did all my own work in the evenings, early mornings and weekends; the quintessential geek on their own at the computer is just my way of working. This obviously changes from project to project, as when I'm working on something architectural I collaborate much more, and with a broader range of people, and on products I work very closely with the makers, which is normally a chain of two or three companies and as many individuals. But I do like having a certain amount of space to myself so that I can explore ideas in a nonverbal way. I have recently begun to work more often in larger design teams, on big civic-scale projects, but luckily this has not diminished the creative space I value so much, of creating intuitively in a private, quiet environment.

I didn't ditch the traditional route on purpose. I've always sent out my CV in the usual way, perhaps with less luck than others because my CV is so odd: if I was looking for an architect to take care of a job, or a draftsman to be solid and follow a project, I would also look at my CV and think, 'What? How are they going to help?' So I ended up gaining employment through other means. For example, one employer was, unbeknownst to me, a follower of mine on Twitter, and she had gained an idea of what I do, how I think and my range of skills from there, and was keen to take me on. Another office that I had applied to many times before took me on when, again unbeknownst to me, someone who had taught me and who I had worked with, and by coincidence had worked with the director of that office before, called him up and gave him the lowdown on me; after the interview went really well, I was in. Then there are the things I have progressed into through competitive selection based on project proposals, like the Designers in Residence at the Design Museum, the Gateways

Top: Folly Ring
Above: Complex
Below: Identity Parade

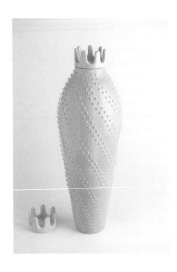

ceramic installation at King's Cross and the British Academy's Rome Prize for Architecture, as well as being awarded an Architectural Association research group to run on colour in architecture and urbanism. In these cases my skill at proposing intriguing briefs came to the fore, and I guess I romanced the juries into going for it; luckily the pudding came out as good proof in each instance for further proposals in the future. Journalism and publishing have proven to be very helpful vehicles. I had always written a lot, and when blogs became popular I began writing a few of those, contributing to friends' blogs. When I wanted to develop my writing further I sent out emails to some magazine editors, and a few of them liked what I had written. I was lucky enough to be able to contribute to the *Architectural Review*, *RIBA Journal*, *Disegno* and *Icon* magazine, among others.

Above: Princex
Below: Proud Little Pyramid
Opposite: New Town tile collection

What happened next

I have been incredibly lucky to see the efforts I have put into my different interests bear fruit in quite wonderful ways. I have published a second book, *Queer Spaces*, teach a master's course at the London College of Communication, and have an exciting stream of work in the public realm that currently includes a 187-foot-long mosaic in London Bridge station, a 177-foot-long artwork in Paddington and the base of a skyscraper in south London, as well as furniture and product ranges for Lebanese, British and Italian brands. At the same time I am still able to create artworks by hand in my studio, illustrations of buildings that I love, a merchandise range that is a joyful side pursuit, and more recently NFTs, which have allowed my digital creations to provide some small income where before there was none. My creative household is busy and noisy and beautiful, and there is no better state in which I could have hoped to move into my forties.

'Diversifiers have to be agile, nimble, proactive go-getters.'

Gem Barton

Dress made from recycled Daler-Rowney
paint tubes, Future Flowers Collection

Don't Get a Job, <u>Make a Job</u>

Strategy:
Swim against the tide
VIN+OMI

With qualifications in geography, anthropology, marketing and photography, and a portfolio of projects covering public art, consultation, fashion design and art direction, talented duo VIN + OMI have experience of almost everything creative and have applied their skills to all these industries successfully.

VIN+OMI have independently and collectively run large public arts organizations, designed and produced 20 large-scale fashion shows and collaborated with more than sixty international companies. They have consulted on renowned design projects and master plans. Sustainability and innovation underpin their work. A realistic view of the different modes of business plays a large part in their decision-making; being creative and being business-minded are not mutually exclusive, as many of the case studies in this book demonstrate. In order to move seamlessly between varied disciplines you need to be agile, flexible, organized and hungry.

'Look at what everyone else is doing and go the other way – seriously. There are too many people following the same path. You are creative – swim the other way.'

Kevin Wilson

Jewellery made from King Charles's recycled plant pots

Experience

Although we set up primarily as a fashion label, we soon decided that the traditional way of showing fashion wasn't for us. The seasonal production of collections is fraught with difficulty and the system of producing fashion in this way produces strains on cash flow and creativity. We decided that focusing only on fashion would not work for us and decided a multi-design process would work. We cross lots of design platforms, directing music videos and a feature film, as well as making public art. We keep ourselves flexible and fluid creatively, and sail hard against traditional fashion models.

We are very sure of our vision and, as a long-term partnership, we have developed a way of discussing our creative ideas. We are not interested in pleasing a fashion audience in terms of fitting into trends or colours – we work outside of the fashion machine. We have found the fashion industry restrictive, and that support is biased towards friends of friends and is heavy on networking. We moved our studio to the Cotswolds in the English countryside to avoid the networking machine and concentrate on what we wanted to do. We collaborate with many other organizations and also act as consultants; we are firm believers that creative brains can do anything creative.

We have purposely honed a wide range of skills between us. We are both artists and marketeers, we design and construct garments. Each of us is computer savvy. We are both paid to consult for other brands and creatives. For some shoots we do the photography, hair and makeup, and we also direct and edit our own and others' videos.

For us, going alone was the only option, as we can do what we like, when we like – you cannot put a price on self-sufficiency. One thing we would say is that if either one of us had tried to do this solo it would not have worked, so for us finding a partner was crucial.

What happened next

Some designers are flagrant networkers and really push social media to the max. We are a little more discreet on social media and I think some of our more successful clients appreciate this.

We don't call ourselves designers but an ideology. Although we started out thinking that traditional fashion was the way, we soon worked on developing our own textiles and our own approach to fashion. Through designing collections via collaborations with other designers and acting as consultants, we decided not to enter traditional fashion retail. We also actively challenged the British Fashion Council model of insisting that new designers have six stockists before they can be considered for inclusion on the schedule for London Fashion Week. We felt that was unsustainable and was the wrong sort of pressure for new designers.

Our non-conformist attitude helped us to develop a much broader approach to design and sustainability. We have always been sustainable and environmentally aware, but no one spoke about it 20 years ago! Following seven years of development, we produced the world's first dress made out of chestnut leather.

One of our higher-profile collaborations was with HM King Charles, then Prince of Wales. We worked with him for three years to explore new ways of developing products from waste materials from his estates, and produced a new textile made from nettles at the Highgrove estate.

We responded to the Covid-19 pandemic and the call for protective masks by producing more than 8,000 eco masks for the NHS, and raised £16,000 from the sale of our five-layer recycled protection masks to the general public. 100 percent of profits went to NHS charities.

Dress made from recycled Daler-Rowney paint tubes, Art Collection

'An awareness and realistic view of the different modes of business are important.'

Gem Barton

Expand your collective language to expand your world

Advice on specialism and diversity from Cruz Garcia and Nathalie Frankowski, WAI Architecture Think Tank

On specialism

Experimentation takes practice. Questioning the status quo and the standard ways of making and thinking requires commitment and continuity. While the questions may take many different approaches, media manifestations and platforms for dissemination and exchange, consistency is generated by developing rigorous working, thinking and producing habits, methods and strategies. Because critical positions may encounter many forms of resistance, it becomes even more important to support and sustain them with tools and strategies of presentation that can be developed through time, without losing continuity and ways to connect projects.

Repetition, commitment and rigour are some of the skills and habits fostered by specialism. Whenever we collaborate with engineers, poets, novelists, philosophers, filmmakers, educators, builders, artists, curators, designers, cultural producers, teachers and architects, it becomes clear that their specialities are what truly contribute to diversity. The most exhilarating forms of collaboration we have experienced involve collectives with people who have dedicated time to develop their skills and their ways of thinking. The more advanced those specialized skills, the stronger the chance to bring something meaningful or alternative to a collective effort. In our practice, the most impactful collaborations have been the ones that allow all of those involved to dig deep into their interests and ways of producing work. Projects are enriched when people can bring their knowledge, generating even deeper connections while creating new networks of knowledge.

Specialism is not only about focusing on a specific task or discipline, but about the rigorous search for ways to engage with a way of thinking or making. To be able to dedicate time to engage with a speciality can allow the exploration of variations, to develop a craft, to improve skills, to be able to make critical assessments by comparison. At the same time, to have a speciality doesn't mean closing all other possibilities, fields of knowledge and production; on the contrary, it demands that alternative channels remain open since there are many ways in which a project can be enriched, and a speciality can be expanded.

On diversity

Diversity is a form of specialism. Knowing that it is not possible to be an expert in everything, it becomes fundamental to understand the importance of continuous questions, collaboration and the free exchange of knowledge. Recognizing when it's time to go beyond a speciality, or when and where to look for answers or directions is a skill that comes from experience. Both of our final projects as students (Cruz in the Universidad de Puerto Rico and Nathalie in Paris La Villette) integrated forms of production that are outside of what is the norm in architecture. One of us developed a theory for the critical use of narratives (Cruz), and the other explored film as a way of storytelling (Nathalie). This way of thinking outside of disciplinary boundaries has been key through our careers. It's something we seek in our collaborations and would advise to our students as they prepare to confront an even more uncertain world. In short, it is to put into practice Ludwig Wittgenstein's aphorism 'the limits of my language mean the limits of my world'. Anti-disciplinarity is a true possibility that can enhance the way we think and operate beyond professionalized constraints and disciplinary boundaries.

As we seek (and need) to expand our worlds, we aim (and would advise) to continuously explore different media, to engage with different thinkers, artists and designers that can bring many specialities and ways of worldmaking. Through the years we have developed a practice that, through very specific questions, has used multimedia, collaborative and anti-disciplinary approaches to question the political, historical and material legacy and imperatives of architecture, urbanism and art through a panoramic and critical approach. If specialism can allow us to invest time to develop craft, skills and ways to interrogate, diversity of media, discourses and approaches can foment further pluriversal forms of worldmaking and collaborations that go beyond disciplinary and professional constraints.

Resilience

Everybody will, at some point, question their progress, their process, and their reasons for being and doing. Each and every person featured in this book – designer, academic and student – will have faced difficult decisions with a potentially life-changing impact. More often than not, this difficult situation becomes a catalyst or motivator for the future. When times are tough, we see the importance in evaluating our goals. This refocusing is a very important part of keeping on track and developing as a person and a designer.

The following featured individuals have had to make tough, life-changing decisions early in their careers. This can be daunting, but by weighing up your options and balancing them with your personal checklist for a happy career, making these tough calls can be the making of you.

Strategy:

Trust your instincts

Jose Garrido

Having the conviction to trust your instincts is an extremely valuable quality to possess at any age. While still at design school, (now) art director and designer Jose Garrido saw the value in working on competition briefs for real clients in his spare time, and fought hard to be allowed to do so during class time too. Submitting proposals to competitions immediately increases the visibility of you and your work, which may be seen by renowned industry professionals on judging panels, by clients themselves and, if conducted well, may be picked up by design blogs and websites with thousands of hits per day. Working to competition briefs shows a dedication to your industry, responsibility, focus and the ability to search out work, follow a brief and keep to deadlines. Being able to talk about well-known brands in a job interview, rather than about generic unnamed student projects, can make for a better flow of conversation and an authentic connection.

Jose decided to leave education, but this kind of decision should not be taken lightly. Jose considered all of his options seriously, spoke at length with his family and decided to take the risk. He was already receiving acclaim for the work he had done, and was being offered the kinds of commission he had once only dreamed of getting after graduation. Getting a head start was the right thing to do for Jose, but it was a risk nevertheless. Every decision we make is a calculated risk, with different odds. You should give your decision the correct amount of consideration, follow your heart, and always have a back-up plan.

BOK COURT VICTORY PUMP II

te: 1987   White/Purple/Blood orange

REEBOK - CANTON, MASSACHUSETTS, USA

Sneaker Coolture project

Experience

It all began when I was selected as an Honourable Mention in the Behance (online platform for showcasing creative work) Student Showdown design competition (2012) with my AVANTH typeface project. I was lucky enough to be chosen along with five other students from more than 1,200 submissions. My work began to be seen on lots of sites and I was contacted by a creative agency in Florida to work freelance for them.

I have always thought that real projects motivate students much more than hypothetical academic exercises. Just swap the brand 'x' in a school assignment for a real brand and you will see how students work harder. Even more so if it is for an actual potential client. I guess that you always aspire to get your work seen in real life, and not just in your class.

When I was in my second year, I saw that a packaging contest was being held by a US brand. I told one of my tutors about it and finally convinced her to set an assignment for it. I ended up doing my best work and was selected as a finalist for my EOS Coffee packaging. After that, lots of publishers contacted me, asking to feature the project in design books. All this from a project used as a school assignment!

'Leaving my degree was a difficult decision, mainly because I wanted to finish it and make my mother proud, but in the end it was the best option, and she understood that. Now she is really proud to see me getting nice jobs and doing what I love.'

Jose Garrido

What happened next

I started contacting a lot of different magazines to ask them if they needed some work. One day I saw that a design studio in New York was looking for a graphic designer and I wrote them an email. They liked my work and I started working with them on some branding projects. My first big client was Gatorade, with whom I collaborated on some typography compositions. At that time I was mostly exploring lettering- and typography-based works that were appealing to certain kinds of client. I came up with a collection project with some recent lettering artworks, which was featured on Behance and then spread through lots of inspiration sites. I suppose people from the Nike team saw them and they contacted me to make two T-shirts.

Above: Nike competition final design and concept image
Below: EOS Coffee packaging

Bronze Mirror

Strategy:

Pivot, make lemonade

Desia Ava (Dessislava Madanska)

Desia Ava has been an entrepreneur since the age of five, when she organized her first 'art auction' selling drawings to the guests who came for dinner at her parents' house. She has always been interested in how things work – not just the creative processes but also the business elements, like sales and communications strategies, so starting her own company, onedesignspace, at 25 was a logical step. More recently, she started her own artist-run independent gallery, Future Space Gallery, uniting international artists in Stockholm.

Midway through her MFA in Spatial Design at Konstfack University of Arts, Crafts and Design in Stockholm, Desia's patience was tested in a way nobody could have expected. While she was taking a trip back home to Bulgaria, the Covid-19 lockdown was announced and she was stranded, away from her studies and away from the work she had spent the last year developing just months before her final submission was due. But in this moment of panic and shock, she pivoted, she trusted her processes and she approached this tough situation in the same way she approaches her art in assembling found objects: with exploration, intuition, contemplation and freedom.

Experience

In April 2020, in the middle of my degree work, I went from Stockholm to Sofia to make a metal cast for a project. That week, the country entered a lockdown, all flights were cancelled, and I was not able to go back to Sweden and finish my project in the way I had planned. After my initial shock and despair, I regrouped and changed my project to fit the current situation. Because of the lockdown, I made objects from materials I had at home, such as pieces of cardboard that I painted black, rope, duct tape, pieces of wood, marble samples, sponges, bricks and wooden branches. With these discarded materials, I created seven pieces, each exploring a different material and representing a different ritual, connected to fire, water and reflection. I decided to focus on rituals in our everyday mundane activities, rather than creating a new religion, to show how important routines are to keep us grounded, especially in times of crisis. Since I was not able to present my work physically to my tutors and classmates, I covered the walls and furniture in my living room with silver foil and turned the space into a 'gallery', filmed a movie of me performing the rituals and shared that on Zoom during my presentation. Later on, the project was featured in the online exhibition 'Don't try this at home' by Antilia Gallery, as well as in a catalogue featuring the exhibition.

My work explores rituals, the cosmic, the eternal beauty of raw materials. My creative process is based on intuitive assembling of objects out of industrial leftover materials and natural artifacts – wood, brass, bronze, marble, travertine, granite and limestone – to create objects that together form spaces for contemplative, meditative

Mist-y Creature

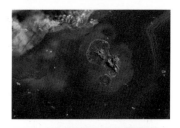

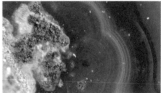

Microcosmic

and mindful experiences. While assembling these peculiar sculptures I am free, liberated. I never know what kind of materials I will find and I don't plan or sketch these objects prior to their making. This signature process gives my work originality and uniqueness.

Every project I create is new to me in terms of technicalities. I never know all the answers when I start; I learn during the making process, sometimes at the cost of many failed tries, but always with the reward that I've learned something new. The most recent example of this empirical approach to my work is a sculpture I am making called Mist-y Creature. It is composed of stainless steel, quartz stones and a mist system. In order to create the mist, I learned about nozzle types, water pressure, water timers, pipe joints and pressure pumps, and I experimented with various configurations until reaching the desired result.

Another project, Microcosmic, is a photographic exploration of crystals and minerals under a microscope. At a scale not visible to the human eye, these images could be interpreted as cosmic formations, topographical landscapes, cells or living organisms, reiterating that all is interconnected in the universe.

Alongside my post-master's research at the Royal Institute of Art in Stockholm, my practice divides currently between experimental art projects and collectable furniture design. In times of challenging economics, I believe that diversification is necessary. However, I find that the best way to do this for me is still to have a connection between the diverse works. In my case, that connection is the exploration of materials and techniques. Often, the techniques and materials I apply to my collectable design objects I also apply in my art practice, and vice versa.

'I never know what kind of materials I will find and I don't plan or sketch these objects prior to their making. This signature process gives my work originality and uniqueness.'

Desia Ava

Don't Get a Job, <u>Make a Job</u>

Strategy:
Take the mic

Marie-Michèle Larivée

With a master's degree in trend forecasting and undergraduate studies in fashion design and management, Quebec-based Marie-Michèle Larivée has an approach that many may believe to be focused on business development rather than design – but foresight requires creative thinking in the same way that designers need vision and imagination. After leaving her steady job with an airline company, taking a leap of faith and applying for a scholarship overseas, she now runs her own consultancy practice in trend analysis and foresight, focusing on the creative industries. She helps creatives foresee their futures, organize research methodologies, and prepare for uncertainties. This may not seem typically 'creative' to some, but it involves designing, reviewing, editing, and most importantly working on open-mindedness, thinking outside the box, and imagining the possibilities beyond existing barriers – the lifeblood of all creative practitioners.

'I read that only about 30 percent of voices in the Canadian media are female.'

Marie-Michèle Larivée

Experience

After completing my bachelor's degree, I left my next step to faith. I applied for a scholarship in Europe, thinking that if I got it, I would leave everything and move overseas for my master's degree, but if I didn't, I would stay in my current job. Well, I got it, so I packed everything and went to Italy for my master's.

I came back to Canada after completing it, but there were no jobs that fitted my expertise and nothing that resonated with what I wanted to do as a career. The Canadian market is a hard one for any work around trend analysis and foresight, because it is fairly unknown and quite different from Europe. Until recently you would never see a posting with a task revolving around trend analysis, forecast or foresight on Canadian soil, or those tasks would only be mentioned as a small part of a position.

I wanted to change trend analysis (I still do) to allow a more ethical and sustainable methodology throughout the foresight process. Taking the leap and becoming freelance/self-employed was an easy decision for me, because there were no positions being offered that suited what I wanted to do. I knew there was a market from an internship I did during my studies and sensed there were contract-based projects more than actual positions to be filled. That's why I built my own business and started to work with clients in the creative industry.

Somewhere down the line of starting my own business, I realized that promoting knowledge and methodology wasn't as aesthetically pleasing as promoting a product, and that I wasn't completely comfortable with solely showcasing my face as a product, since my service is to help companies understand their futures. It involves a lot of information, intuition and collective knowledge, and it is far from being based just on myself.

I also came across a statistic that made me want to contribute my voice to the media and on stage, when I read that only about 30 percent of voices in the Canadian media are female. That kept me going in terms of commenting in the media and encouraged me to help other women and female-identifying and non-binary people around me to take the mic and speak about their fields of expertise.

Advice

To gain a better understanding of international and interconnected markets I have joined a number of communities, including Global Scanning Network by Copenhagen Institute of Future Studies (CIFS) and TW:IN by trendwatching. Being in communities, units and groups, especially the international ones, gave me access to innovation and emerging practices from around the globe, as well as different ways of doing business and potential clients. I even hired someone in an online community to work with on a research project! It is great to chat and bounce ideas around with people with different points of view, especially for forecasting-related work, which is still very under-represented.

Top: Desk research
Above: Trend analysis and foresight materials

'Being in communities and groups, especially international ones, gave me access to innovation and emerging practices from around the globe.'

Marie-Michèle Larivée

Build best-case scenarios in your imagination

Advice on facing tough calls from Jimenez Lai, Bureau Spectacular

One of my favourite thought exercises is the projection of multiple futures. It is about revisiting your personal past and constructing branches of five, six or seven possible futures. What decisions have I made in my life that have led up to this moment? This thought crosses my mind during moments of intense trouble or pleasure. If every fork in the road leads to either a path of happiness or one of regret, it is comforting to remind ourselves that alternate timelines exist. No matter what we choose, a future on the other side of that fork in the road happened. That reality exists – it is just not ours. There is no sense in stewing in regret because your best hopes and wishes exist in that other world out there.

With this knowledge in mind, we can pre-emptively construct these plural paths. Is it possible to open an exhibition next year? Can I be friends with these people I admire? Will I move to a city of my liking, working in exactly the ways I would otherwise envy? The answer is always yes to every possible future. If you have the courage to build a best-case scenario timeline in your imagination, that reality is already as good as real.

I lived in a desert shelter at Taliesin, Arizona, in 2004, and resided in a shipping container on the piers of Rotterdam at Atelier Van Lieshout in 2005. During those years, my relationship with material goods transformed, as I realized I did not need many of the societal norms I was brought up to 'need'. I subsequently began intensely compartmentalizing my life, reducing all that is personal to an extremely low proportion, and spent the majority of my time in production mode. I published my first book entitled *Citizens of No Place* with Princeton Architectural Press in 2012. In 2014 I was the designer and curator for the Taiwan Pavilion at the Venice Architecture Biennale. I also had the great pleasure of being in the permanent collection at the Museum of Modern Art with my installation work *White Elephant*, and seven of my accompanying drawings for that project.

I am currently a professor at the school of architecture at UCLA.

Many of my first projects were self-initiated. Nobody commissioned me at the beginning. I subscribed to the 'if you build it, they will come' business model instead of the 'show me the money' train of thought. I felt that I needed some years of building up a strong argument about why I like what I like, and in that way I would not need to compromise my time and efforts. To begin, I was able to sustain my life and my work by teaching at universities and getting grants.

My advice is to write a few 'fake' CVs for versions of your future selves – let your ambition run wild, project a few futures. No one is watching, there is no need to feel ashamed about these fake futures. I promise you, as you print them and hold your plural futures in your hands, you will gain a deep sense of clarity about what you want to do and what you do not care to do.

Don't Get a Job, <u>Make a Job</u>

Going it alone and teaming up

What are the options and how do you know what's right for you? After years of instruction, direction, rules and regulations at college or university, for many the thought of being your own boss, making your own decisions/mistakes and taking charge of your own future may be preferable.

Barriers to entry into the creative industries have never been so low. This means entering this market as a new graduate can be smooth, which is a great thing for young entrepreneurs and collaborative groups. In order to take that step, it is important to carefully consider your options, but at some point the thinking has to stop and the doing has to start. Be smart about things, but don't let worries of profit margins and contracts stop you before you have started.

But what about the risks involved? Could teaming up with like-minded individuals be an option? There can be strength in numbers, feelings of warmth and support, bubbling excitement from being deep inside the hubbub – a sense that together you can achieve anything.

The following case studies illustrate the full breadth of the spectrum, from one-woman bands to free-form collectives.

Branson Aquarium Kaleidoscope

Strategy:

Listen to your inner passion

Tina Fung

Tina Fung is the principal set designer and artist at Space Objekt, a Singapore-based boutique design studio that is reshaping understanding of built environments and reimagining spatial experiences. Tina knows the value of working solo, and of when, with whom and how to collaborate. Although her journey has not been straightforward, her early years studying interior design and a later pivot back to the visual arts have seen her generate an incredibly rich practice, one she is rightly proud of.

Experience

As a young adult, I wanted to study visual arts, but it was never an option for me as, in the eyes of Asian parents, it was not viewed as a sustainable career. I studied interior design instead, which was perceived as a more valid career choice. Growing up, my extra-curricular activities revolved around the creative arts. I took after-school classes in everything from dance to music, painting to life drawing, weaving to sculpting, pottery to photography – the list goes on. I believe that this played a huge role in where I am today.

After graduating from Chelsea College of Art & Design with a BA and an MA, I started working as an interior designer. I did it for ten years, and it brought me to Singapore. But the job wasn't giving me the creative satisfaction I was looking for. It wasn't until I made my first trip to Burning Man, where I was surrounded and inspired by countless pieces of art, that I realized I needed to pursue my

Mahkota, Malay Heritage Centre

Labradoresence, Summer Well

inner urge of creating art. My journey began when I made the career shift to working as a set designer for the Singapore nightclub Zouk.

My role at Zouk allowed me to use the venue as a blank canvas to explore and create installations. This was heavily supported by the founder, who was an avid art collector. It was a great platform to showcase my work and to experiment with different methods in creating immersive art installations.

I now have my own studio, Space Objekt. My portfolio includes installations for lifestyle brands such as Gucci, Sephora, Grab, DBS Bank, Prudential, Red Bull and Ultra Music Festival Singapore, plus an interior design project for Wyllow. I have diversified into film set design for the likes of Jasmine Sokko, Universal Studios Singapore and many more. Additionally, I'm a TEDx speaker and have shared my personal journey and ideas about the importance of shareable art through social media.

Gynoid, Zoukout Festival

In a way, things have come full circle. My point is that passion is important. Every journey I have made as a creative has helped pave the way to where I am now. Had my passion, self-belief or aspirations not been present, there would have been a slightly different outcome.

For me, collaboration is about building a stronger voice, making connections, fostering kinship and exploring different perspectives to my own work. In the real world, you never really work completely alone. Even as an artist working on solo commissions, it is inevitable that you will be required to work with different teams such as curators, organizers, vendors, brands and venues.

Part of my process when working alone includes seeking feedback from friends, fellow creatives, artists or designers because, after looking at the work for so long, it can be easy to get wound up in it and not be able to look at it as a bigger picture. So it's important to put it in front of people who you respect.

As I've grown and evolved over the years, I have learned what my strengths and weaknesses are, so when I do join forces with someone who specializes in something completely different, the outcome is much better. It really opens up a new perspective, and I like to offer something in return too. I have collaborated with myriad creatives from different backgrounds, including motion designers, illustrators, sound producers and engineers. My hope is to collaborate with creatives who haven't necessarily seen their work in three-dimensional space and make art accessible to everyone.

'Part of my process when working alone includes seeking feedback from friends, fellow creatives, artists and designers.'

Tina Fung

Wyllow store, Los Angeles

Strategy:

Don't run before you can walk

State of Play

Like many other ambitious young creatives, Luke Whittaker was unfulfilled by his post-university work experiences. Wanting more control over his own career, he leapt into the world of freelancing and has never looked back.

He entered the field of video-game design during a time of economic downturn. Even potential investors questioned his timing, but this was not something that concerned Luke, perhaps because the video-games industry is one that has continued to grow regardless. Being aware of the world around you, and understanding your chosen market and your position within it, is key to surviving. Being a sole trader with minimal overheads can be a big plus here – you can react quickly to changing tides, free of the restraining costs and worries associated with running a large firm.

Early growth as an individual or a small company is of course important, but growing too fast, taking on too many jobs, contributors and commitments can be very dangerous. As incoming fees and payments may be staggered and sporadic, while outgoings are regular and expanding, many young firms that grow too fast can find themselves in trouble financially. Be aware of your trajectory, choose your projects carefully (it is OK to turn down inappropriate work), and don't run before you can walk.

South of the Circle

'I knew it was a gamble but I'd had requests coming in for work.'

Luke Whittaker

Experience

While at university I did work experience as a runner for a special effects company in Soho, thinking that I loved animation and films, but I discovered that it had inherited the structure of the film and TV industry. You needed to prove yourself for years at the bottom before anyone would let you do anything interesting. I remember being asked to leave a room by a senior producer because I was showing an interest in an animator's work. I felt that the hierarchy strangled any creativity and fun.

I was fortunate to get my first job at a web-design company that was a little understaffed, which meant I had to do a lot myself. I learned to program and be self-sufficient, and within a year I went freelance. Some of my university work had been noticed, and that helped give me a boost.

Deciding to go it alone didn't seem like a tough decision at all – I knew it was a gamble but I'd had requests coming in for work while I was still employed in my first job, so felt reasonably confident that there was work out there. I made sure I saved about three months' wages and then gave myself the challenge of seeing if it would get off the ground within that time.

My university work, A Break in the Road, won a couple of awards. I put it on the internet for people to play for free and suddenly it went everywhere, with people emailing it to friends as this was before Facebook and Twitter. I ended up with a huge bill from my hosting company as I'd gone over my limit, so my first success was also a financial disaster! But it did get the work in front of thousands, and clients got in touch; I created a whole new version for Shockwave, and MTV asked me to make a music-based game for them and I could make what I wanted and name a budget. At the time it seemed like the dream job, but now we invest our own money into the games, which is a little more risky but gives us even more control.

I freelanced for five years, occasionally working with a programmer or sound designer. I can do both, but I've learned not to take on too much: I'm an artist mainly, and other people are often far more qualified at the other disciplines. In 2008, I set up State of Play with my wife, which meant that we had a structure to employ others and create something bigger than just me. In the end there's only a certain amount that you can do yourself, especially with games that demand such a great amount of technical and artistic integration.

Initially we worked on smaller projects, giving us a large amount of creative control. There are huge triple-A video games being made out there, but if you work for those companies you're likely only doing a small part of a large project. Being independent allowed us to explore and develop our own style, with our own ideas, and not need to fit into anyone else's plans.

Advice

I think having a great project that you can show to people when you graduate is massively important, or a body of good work plus a good website to show it off professionally. The website doesn't need to be complicated, just clear and simple.

I would recommend giving yourself a financial cushion of a few months if you can, as it means that you're starting under less pressure, which is good for your state of mind and probably helps you to assess where you're going more clearly. If you need to team up, it's a good idea to get an agreement in writing if possible, then everyone knows what's expected.

I didn't have a firm business plan, and still don't, only a conviction to keep doing better work and keep the spirit of creativity alive. You can't predict exactly what will happen in the business world, but you can guide yourself through the changes with a sense of purpose. For example, we were making web games in 2009, but in 2010 the iPad came out and completely changed things – nobody knew if that would be a success or a failure. But it's given us even more creative freedom, even more control

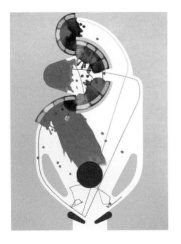

Above and below right:
South of the Circle
Below left: INKS

over publishing, and allowed us to create bigger and better projects. If we had had a business plan in 2009 we'd have had to rip it up!

If you can make the conditions right and not tie yourself to too many other pressures, then following your nose and intuition can be really rewarding. It's pretty much what being creative is all about.

What happened next

Our game Lumino City won a BAFTA for Artistic Achievement. The next game, INKS, picked up an Apple Design Award, and the next, KAMI 2, was nominated for a BAFTA. With each one, we allowed time for the team to experiment, keeping alive the spirit that founded the company, and allowing our instincts to drive us forward. We also developed a process: stay a small team with low costs while experimenting, grow bigger during production to get the game made efficiently. This has helped us face some big challenges. Earnings for paid-for games on mobile, traditionally our most successful platform, have fallen. But we've been able to adapt and have become more ambitious.

Our latest game, South of the Circle, is a fully motion-captured narrative adventure set in Cold War Antarctica for mobile, consoles and PC. This is the first game for which we've had funding due to its ambitious scale, but we stressed the need to keep our creative freedom. I travelled to Antarctica for research, to work on the art, the story and the creative direction, and members of our team were similarly involved in multiple disciplines. The aim is still to keep State of Play an innovative place, to foster the freedom we started out with.

'I think having a great project that you can show to people when you graduate is massively important.'

Luke Whittaker

Designs for the opera *A Dream of Armageddon*

Strategy:
Family matters
werkstattkollektiv

Lisa Kentner, Marie Gerstenberger, Vivien Waneck, Malena Modéer, Dorothea Andrae-Kuttner, Ulrike Plehn and Rebekka Grimm are more of a family than a collective. As the right working concept did not exist for them, they had to create their own, and werkstattkollektiv, based out of Berlin, has grown organically ever since. After meeting when studying costume design at the Universität der Künste, Berlin, almost twenty years ago, they are now a successful and eclectic association of costume and stage designers, stylists and decorators, wardrobe masters, scenery and costume painters. They design and manufacture costumes, rooms, figures and objects. They can fully equip a production, from concept to implementation, or work separately on commissions and custom orders that are part of a production. Their size and variation in skills and interests across these sectors allows them to morph and change based on each project, although it isn't always plain sailing.

Experience

We've known each other for many years now, but our 'teaming up' was part of a journey, and the idea of having our own company for costume and set design and custom-made costumes, objects and artworks developed over the years. The process is not finished yet: we still try to find the right structures for us without hierarchy but with different responsibilities. We are very different characters with different talents and specializations, and that makes us very strong as a company. We can support each other, especially in difficult times or projects.

Also special about our constellation is the fact that we are seven women and over the years we've happened to have 12 children, between 1 and 14 years old. Being self-employed with kids is tough, but our collective helps us to be able to work in this business with no regular working hours. It also helps to buffer us against sudden illnesses, accidents and unexpected complications. During parental leave, none of us had to be afraid of losing clients because the others could take over.

When we finished studying, none of us wanted to go down the classic path of costume design, which would have meant travelling around the German theatrical landscape alone. We all have a love for the craft, so we decided to fill a gap between art/design and craft. In practice, this often means being the one who finds solutions for very specific problems. The collective gives us the chance to take on very different jobs because each one of us is particularly good at something. That way it never gets boring. At the same time, however, there is sometimes a lack of calm and reflection when we are at our busiest.

Below: Sleepfairy
Bottom: Costume created for Ruhrtriennale's Bählamms Fest

Our first projects came to us through word of mouth. Someone knew someone who had heard what we were doing and could use our work. That hasn't changed to this day. We're not very good at advertising and presenting ourselves; I suppose it is more a word-of-mouth situation.

The most obvious advantage of a collective is not being alone in a not very secure work field. It is good to push each other and to remember the good things in times of doubt. The creative potential is much bigger in a group, and of course we offer fast access and a large capacity of womanpower. On the other hand, there can be difficulties when the framework is so flexible, as you have to clarify nearly every day what is fair: fair working conditions, fair work distribution, fair salary, fair solution of everyday problems. In the end it is like a big family. You have wonderful times but also struggles.

Our biggest adventure together so far was our relocation. We rented a 1,076-foot-square industrial hall with walls and a roof, but nothing else. Thanks to a very gracious landlord, we were allowed to do almost anything we wanted. After long discussions and hundreds of phone calls we invented a space that suits everyone and will be a beautiful place to be and work. We had to do everything – windows, electricity, water. But we got great help and support from friends and family. It was exhausting, but it was worth it, and it proved once again that we can achieve anything together!

Above: Design for *Don Quichotte*
Below: Design for *The Magic Flute*

'Our collective helps us to be able to work in this business with no regular working hours.'

werkstattkollektiv

Yardhouse

Strategy:

Feel your way

Assemble

Assemble is a non-hierarchical fun-commune of young creatives with a clever approach to making dreams come true, proving in their early days that, contrary to popular belief, experience isn't everything – if you work hard, trust in each other and follow your noses, true success really can come your way.

There is no predetermined recipe for such a foray into design and business; having life goals, a business plan and company manifesto are all worthy productions, but when you are stepping outside of the typical freelance/sole-trader box, there has to be some feeling-in-the-dark first. For the first year or so, the now-named Assemble were not registered as a company, and did not have a bank account, or even a name!

For some, being involved in forward-thinking design is their dream; for others being innovative is embedded so deep in their genetics that everything they do becomes a new and exciting experience. The Assemblers would not have been content working for somebody else, in a traditional setting, format and structure – for them this would have been too restricting. They need to have choice and control, luxuries that conventional employment cannot provide them with.

In 2015 Assemble won the prestigious Turner Prize for their project in Liverpool's Granby Four Streets – a revitalization of buildings and community through design that had been ignored and disenfranchised. They were the first architecture or design studio to receive the prize. Their book *Collaboration* reflects on the collaborative strategies developed over their ten-year history, seen as an ongoing documentation of their approach to making, material, authorship and collective practice, and is a great read for anyone considering a similar pathway. Matthew Leung reveals their experience on the following pages.

'Our economy was one of many hands – working together was not only desirable, but necessary.'

Assemble

Below and opposite, right: Folly for a Flyover, **Opposite, left:** The Cineroleum

Experience

The collective nature of Assemble is its defining characteristic. Working together in a non-hierarchical group is, in many ways, the most logical approach, and allows us to share responsibility, pool knowledge and be productive. The mechanisms of this kind of practice are subject to constant renegotiation and have gradually evolved in the 13 years since our first collective endeavour, the Cineroleum on London's Clerkenwell Road.

Imagined as a marriage of two typologies in decline in city centres – the picture palace and the petrol station – this temporary project had no client, no budget and no particular reason for being. It was dreamed up as a means of realizing a collective urge to build. In the evenings and weekends over several months, the project was slowly developed; the necessary permissions were sought, materials were gathered, plans were drawn. Armed with a minimal range of tools, holiday days and unpaid leave (and eventually a small grant from Ideas Tap), our economy was one of many hands – working together was not only desirable, but necessary.

Nowhere was this more evident than in the construction of the Cineroleum project itself. Aside from the structure for the seating rake, which was put up by a scaffolding company, we built every element with the aid of enthusiastic friends, family, and new acquaintances made along the way. The silver curtain was made from breather membrane, obtained for free and pleated with domestic sewing machines. Wooden flip-up seats were fabricated from reclaimed scaffolding boards, and old school furniture received new inlaid formica marquetry tops. Each screening required almost every member of the group – around twenty of us – to be present, to project the film, stamp tickets, staff the bar and, most importantly, to hoist the curtain at the end of each film to reveal the city to the audience.

At that time, with much of the group in full-time employment or education, there was little thought given to the idea that this way of working could form the basis of an alternative form of practice – there was no expectation of employment or payment, or even future projects. The Cineroleum was simply fun. The output of the collective over this period has been equally diverse, ranging from research projects to travelling exhibitions, temporary theatres to public realm improvements, housing to workshops, playgrounds to art galleries, and workspace buildings to furniture. This variety reflects the relatively large size of the collective, but also the diversity of interests within the group. There is a common preoccupation with making and the social context of design, but the general rule is that any project, regardless of type, size or budget, is of interest if any two people feel strongly about it and are willing to take it forward.

In this way, each member works in a freelance capacity, often on a number of different projects simultaneously; it has not been practical, or even desirable, for the whole group to work on each new project in the same manner as for the Cineroleum or the Folly for a Flyover. Instead, we have retained the ideal of a flat hierarchy, but work as individuals and smaller teams who have freedom within, and can draw on the support of, the collective.

Advice

There are many talented and well-connected designers out there who will do well on their own, but for us the collective spirit was what made projects possible. Finding other like-minded individuals is key. I would also suggest that you do everything yourself at the beginning – book-keeping, meetings, clearing up, building, drawings – it is important that you have some kind of understanding of all aspects of practice as well as the life of the things you design.

Chair Arch, Queenstown, New Zealand

Strategy:

The more true to yourself, the better

The Glue Society

The Glue Society is not an advertising agency but a creative collective of writers, designers, artists and directors who believe that concept and execution can be brought together in the same creative space, blurring the lines between art and commerce.

The whole is greater than the sum of its parts – having a team on hand to bat ideas around with, to make coffee for, to share stories, to offer up alternatives, to challenge and to spur on is priceless. It also means that you can take on more work, spreading risk and tapping more than one field or genre. Not to mention the vibe and the camaraderie that can lift every person in any situation.

When starting a collective, it is important to set out a shared goal, a mission statement or similar, summarizing who you are, who you want to be and the ethos behind the work you hope to produce. Once you have decided this (it could take years to refine), it is important that each member is on board, always striving for the same goal – be true to this goal with every step. On the following pages, Jonathan Kneebone describes the collective's experience.

Experience

Below: It Wasn't Meant to End Like This, Aarhus, Denmark; bottom: Knowledge Keeps Like Fish

The advertising industry has a very particular and well-trodden career path that you are encouraged to go down. You start as a junior writer or art director and work your way up via group head to executive creative director and ultimately, perhaps, to having your name on the door of your own agency. The only issue with this traditional route is that the higher up the ladder you go, the fewer opportunities you tend to get to actually be creative. You often end up in meetings, steering the ship, but not actually making things or getting any chance to get your hands dirty. This is what motivated us to look for an alternative solution. The result was to start our own creative collective, working on a project basis for both agencies and clients, which allowed us to both conceive and execute ideas.

We believe that working together can create a result far greater than any individual could deliver. One example of this is the TV show we developed and directed called *Watch with Mother*. Asked by the public broadcaster in Australia to create a new piece of entertainment, we came back to them with various ideas. However, our first attempts were perhaps more conventional than they had expected. What they were interested in was something that only we could have created, something that took

our approach to commercial creativity and brought it into the broadcasting world.

We worked as a group on a concept and realized that our own brand of creativity would necessarily disorientate the audience in order to get them more deeply involved. The idea we subsequently pitched was for a sketch horror show – a world first, something only we could have come up with.

We took the concept of regular characters from a sketch show format but gave each of the personalities very dark habitual behaviours. The result was a highly experimental six-part series, which managed to simultaneously freak people out and make them laugh. To make the show affordable and capable of being produced in a two-week period, each of the team at the Glue Society took responsibility for writing and directing different sketches. As a result we ended up with something that no one person would have been capable of. The show was released online and ran on SBS in Australia. In many ways it has given each of us the confidence to bring that freshness and experimentation into our work.

'Proving that there is such a thing as conventional behaviour is a very motivating reason to do something new.'

Jonathan Kneebone

Tendedero, Santiago, Chile

Another aspect of our creative output is in the area of installations or activations, where brands express themselves through actions not words. These activations tend to impact not one but two audiences: both the people who experience the work first hand – in person – and those who experience the work via social channels or shareable content.

What we have realized, particularly during the pandemic, when fewer live experiences were possible, is that both audiences matter. You have to create something that excites and inspires the primary audience, but you also have to delight the secondary audience with something that gives them a taste of the experience, because the secondary audience is potentially enormous. You have to provide them with something that makes them feel as if they have some realization or observation from a distance.

This led us to realize the power of a central core image – something that in one instance communicates almost everything. If you can get this right, then the image will be shared all around the world almost of its own accord. This impacts the way we tend to develop work. In some ways, it has become a common thread linking all our work.

A good example of this is the Grave of Thrones concept, when we helped DDB in Sydney to promote the final season of the show *Game of Thrones* for Foxtel/HBO by creating a graveyard for all the dead characters from across the series. It had to work for both local visitors and those just viewing on Instagram.

We are keen to involve the audience in our work and, in some respects, to start a conversation with them through a subtle disorientation. We now find people come to us to help them develop their own ideas so that they include this dimension.

Watch with Mother

HBO/Grave of Thrones, Sydney

Advice

The best advice I personally was given came from Paul Arden, when he was Creative Director at Saatchi & Saatchi. He simply encouraged me to work out who I was, and then to express that. To some extent, that is where we now find ourselves. As a collective we are at a point where we are applying our own brand of creativity to the problems we are being asked to develop, build, direct or make.

Just being yourself sounds easy, but in reality you have to work at it. There are so many demands placed on you that sometimes you suppress what you really feel in order to do what you think the client or creative director wants of you. But the truer you are to yourself, the more original your work will be. The more true to yourself you can be, the better.

If you think of any famous artist, writer, filmmaker, sculptor or musician, you can almost recognize their style by their work. You can spot a piece by Banksy or Wolfgang Tillmans; there is a strong sense of the individual behind the work. It's something that great directors also do. In some respects, advertising could do with more people who have this aspiration.

We once asked different creative people why they liked to break convention. Stephen Fry replied, 'to prove that it exists'. It wakes people up to the fact that things that are different are actually inspiring and wonderful. For us, the desire to break new ground gets us up in the morning. We are most alive when we are doing something that has never been done before. When you have that as a creative principle, it can't help but also influence your attitudes to career and life in general. It becomes both addictive and inspiring. *Creativity* magazine recently defined us with an expression that we wish we'd thought of ourselves: 'The Glue Society are the experts at things that haven't been done before.'

Go it alone or team up?

Advice on solo working and collaboration by Gem Barton

If doing group work at school or university brings back memories of arguing, ego trips and design-by-committee outcomes, then maybe the idea of a collaborative practice isn't for you. On the other hand, if these situations brought out the best in you as well as those you were working with, allowing everybody to work to their strengths, then maybe joining forces with others equal to but different from you might be exactly what you need.

In reality, working life is of course different to any educational experience in terms of goals, values, practices and parameters, but it can tell you a lot about whether solo working or team working is a suitable environment for you. Bear in mind, this might not remain the same throughout your creative journey; it may fluctuate based upon the type of work, the type of client, your level of experience, and the state of the economy.

Here are some important questions to ask yourself if considering going it alone and setting up your own venture:

Who are you? How do you want to be seen? What will your identity be?

Company name and brand identity are important parts of your 'optics', so getting this right early is essential. It can be tough to change a name and brand once you have built up a reputation, so take some time to get this right before you launch.

Do you have the experience and information you need to be confident in your decision to go it alone now?

Do your research and get experience of things you think might be fundamental to your success before doing them for yourself.

How will you keep a healthy work/life balance? Who is your support system?

Make sure you have a community around you, or even a mentor, to offer support and advice in the difficult times but also to celebrate alongside when those big wins come in!

Here are some important questions to ask yourself if considering teaming up in a more collaborative way:

Do you have the same values and views on where you are headed creatively?

It can be good to brainstorm this collectively ahead of any official launch, even put something down in writing. This will likely be important information for anyone wanting to work with you too, and could take the form of a manifesto or a mission statement on your website.

What is the balance of skills?

One of the core benefits of working as a collective is that you each bring something different to the table. When formulating your working 'family', try to ensure that you have the right mix of skills, interests, abilities, knowledge and talent. Having too many people competing for the same opportunities, and nobody wanting to do certain things, can leave huge holes in your workload and cause real tensions. If there are certain skills that nobody in the team has, it is sensible to agree in advance that these things will be outsourced, or that one member will learn how to do it themselves, saving precious money.

How will you allocate tasks, opportunities and money?

It can be difficult to talk about fairness and money at the start of a joint endeavour, but this is the best time to do it. Be sure that you have a process in place to ensure that all collaborative members have fair and equal access to the opportunities, that all parties do their fair share of the jobs or tasks that they are capable of, and that remuneration reflects contribution.

Gusto

To deviate from tradition takes that special something; the determination, the drive, the passion to take risks and do things differently simply because it would be harder to live with the 'not knowing'.

Don't make the obvious decisions – choose the least travelled path and surprise yourself in every way. Life will always throw you curve balls; these 'unexpecteds' are the deviation from the norm, the happy sprinkles of oddity that make life lively. The trick is not just to be aware of their existence; you need to seek them out, even taunt them, and challenge them to find you.

Have big ideas and don't be afraid of them. Nurture your weirdest ideas, feed them, water them, and let them grow into wild and wondrous things that no one else could ever dream of.

The following case studies illustrate some of the benefits that you can hope to experience with a combination of fearless positivity, an unbending enjoyment of your chosen field, guts and determination.

Strategy:
Don't wait for things to happen
Mega

The French art director and illustrator known only as Mega has gone to extremes to make his dreams come true. He places no limitations on himself and he truly believes that he can achieve anything. This degree of positivity, belief, determination and willpower has served him well. He has undertaken things many others would never attempt: traversing the globe, telling little white lies to befriend important people (though of course we would never sanction breaking the law). Mega did what he had to do to get his foot in the door, and he was bold and cheeky with it. He was remembered.

He wanted to art-direct publications, so he did. He wrote his own book of his experiences and findings in New York. He didn't rely on anyone else, he didn't wait for someone to give him a job – he made his own. He created the project to showcase his skills and his knowledge, and on the back of this he was hired to art-direct other magazines. Clients and employees want to know that you can do the job and do it well, and have examples and proof to show them – Mega made sure he had these. This resolve and tenacity gave him the stepping-stone he needed to jump from working in a fast-food restaurant to running his own business. In this new role as an art director Mega noticed that freelance illustrators were often unreliable, so he turned something that could have been a trial into an opportunity and produced the artwork himself, all the while keeping the clients happy and extending his own skill base and portfolio. Being able to spot niches in the market, identify opportunities and close in on them before everyone else has had their breakfast is priceless. Be active, be busy, do things!

Lezilus Megastore

Experience

While at art school, I had no money but wanted to do things. I worked for six months in a burger restaurant in order to collect the money to buy a ticket to New York, where I went to the offices of all the people that I wanted to meet (record labels, skateboard companies, brand headquarters). I would just knock on doors and pretend to be a journalist in order to meet and interview the different actors of the so-called New York underground scene. It worked. Enthusiasm was my credibility – people would open up to me and I even ended up becoming friends with some of them. Back in France I worked a lot and produced a book called *NYC Rules*, a pretty ambitious graphic design project about the Big Apple's alternative scenes. Then I went to all of the magazine offices, with no appointment, presented what I had done, and gave them a copy of the book (everybody likes free stuff). All of the important media talked about my project and soon I was hired to become the art director of a French publication. This was the beginning of my career in the industry. People at my art school were still talking, but I was doing.

'Being able to spot niches in the market ... and close in on them before everyone else ... is priceless.'

Gem Barton

Below left: illustration for
Men's Health
Right: illustration for *Complex*

Capture d'écran

What happened next

Working as an art director for magazines means being in charge of the visual aspect. I would have to find illustrators or photographers to illustrate the articles given to me by the editor. The biggest problem is that many people don't respect deadlines, and I had to wait for them before I could do my layout. I quickly realized that if you want something done, you'd better do it yourself. This is how I started replacing late visuals with my own illustrations in the magazines I worked for. I began to be noticed as an illustrator, and other magazines began ordering my artwork for their own titles.

'Don't wait for things to happen – you are the one who can create your opportunities. Draw the art you want to see, create the events you want to attend, write the books you want to read.'

Mega

Strategy:

Work smart and take risks

Jordan Jackson

Ever since selling his old clothes and toys from his father's garage at nine years old, Jordan has been driven to explore the world of business, having figured out in elementary school that college was not the route for him. Now, at 19, he is the owner of Birch & Pen, and is the youngest ever store owner in Charleston, South Carolina. Originally from Baltimore, Maryland, he was exposed to a lot of successful entrepreneurs and wanted that stability and freedom for his own family. He studied great entrepreneurs and learned that the key is to work smarter and take risks. Jordan has worked, and continues to work, incredibly smartly, taking risks and learning from his past while at the same time supporting other young people, spreading joy – and breaking records too.

Experience

I've been experimenting in the retail space since I was 17. I started with an online clothing store and used influencer marketing to grow it. Then I went back to the drawing board and began to focus on my big dream of having a physical store. When I first started, I used what I had access to. Thankfully, my mother used to help people to build and grow their businesses and she was a great resource. I visited and toured many locations just to see them face to face and to make my dream more realistic. I opened my store and launched Birch & Pen. I hired underdogs who were driven but couldn't really get opportunities from other companies even if they were qualified. That was crazy to me, but I believed in them and their abilities. Now I'm working on rebranding and scaling my company. I'm excited about it!

Socially, I feel that I wasn't understood by my peers while growing up. I do think my childhood prepared me for experiences that I have lived so far as a young Black man. Even when I opened Birch & Pen, I had to mentally prepare myself for that role and the mission that God gave me, especially with the significant traction that my story gained. Over 10 million people shared my story on social media, along with thousands of locals who were ready to support me. But with those many great experiences came some people who didn't have my best interests at heart. I had to learn when to say no to certain opportunities and when to drown out the noise to refocus on what was important, which was making my dream and my business work. I know for sure that tunnel vision came from my childhood.

Advice

I've had many great experiences. However, I have to fight a ton of obstacles. It can be emotionally draining when you are presented with wonderful opportunities and they don't go through, but it does give me the drive to push even harder. There are also a lot of disparities that come with the territory of being a young Black man that can be very challenging, but it's worth pushing through if it will make the journey a little easier for the next person. Personally, I only work on projects that will make a difference somehow, even if it's not immediate. I do believe that one day I will succeed!

I want everyone to know that it is possible to follow their dreams and bet on themselves.

'I had to learn when to say no to certain opportunities and when to drown out the noise to refocus on what was important.'

Jordan Jackson

Strategy:

Make the 'everyday' beautiful

Sandra Junker

Sandra Junker is a tenacious and hardworking Mainz-based multi-disciplinary conceptual artist working across photography, design, digital art, and everything in between. She is the founder of Studio SeeYa, crafting eye-catching visuals and corporate identities to help brands stand out from the crowd through the power of her images. Sandra studied communication design at the University of Darmstadt and at Camberwell College of the Arts in London, as well as earning a degree in product and advertising photography. She started Studio SeeYa straight out of university, landing her first project while in the dentist's chair. Now she specializes in rebranding 'everyday' businesses: the tax advisor, the salesman, the swimming school. She also has a separate, more artistic practice, where she uses her skills to highlight important issues such as consumer behaviours and fast fashion.

Campaign for OhSheSells

Gusto 151

'I took a leap … my first job was starting my own business.'

Sandra Junker

Branding for dentist
Katrin Wernstedt

Experience

Before studying, I was a trainee photographer. Most of the time I was working hands-on in a photo studio, and every four weeks I would spend two weeks at school to learn the theoretical part of photography. During this time, I had already realized that I never wanted to be an employee again. I wanted to make my own decisions and to deal with the consequences directly. So I took a leap; I didn't get any work experience, and my first job was starting my own business.

I've learned that networking is one of the true keys to being successful. People need to know that you exist and what you can do for them. While I was studying, I thought people would find me. I dreamed of being an overnight success. That *can* happen, but it didn't happen to me. I forced myself to go to events such as exhibition openings and lectures each week. I always went alone, so I was forced to talk to strangers, learning that it's not always with the intention of getting a job, but more to widen your circle. Through this I learned to get to know many inspiring people.

I questioned if I could really start my own studio right after university, as I only had conceptual art projects in my portfolio. I didn't know how to start, and overthinking it made me hesitate, until one day I just asked my dentist during a treatment. I said that I would love to redesign her branding and website. And she said yes! This is how I landed my first 'big' design job without any proper examples in my portfolio. This project gave me the boost I needed to start many more projects, and when there are things that I don't know, I ask for help. Now I spend my time helping 'everyday' businesses show how special they are, helping them to stand out in a mundane and busy world.

In order to attract the 'right' kind of clients, I learned quickly that my own website needed to reflect me, my style, my process and my approach. Since I changed my branding to better reflect myself, I've started to attract the 'right' clients, but you do not always get to choose who you work for. Sometimes I have to make compromises and combine more traditional ways with my style and my ideas. The key is to find a balance. Rejecting a job isn't easy, especially when you need the money. But in the end, it was worth it. Wasting energy on jobs you are not enjoying takes up so much of your energy; I found I couldn't focus enough on the jobs I really loved working on.

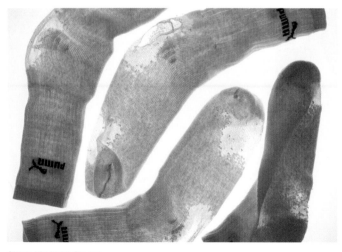

Show Me Your Closet

That's also why my customers come to me: 'I want to stand out and want something different!' That's how tax consultant Christian Wiesner approached me, for example. Tax consultants usually have rather plain and inconspicuous branding. Now, on his website, rockets are launched, a light goes on in a brain, or a sculpture is refined. This and other parts of the branding can be found everywhere in his tax office now.

Not all the things I am interested in sit inside a corporate model, so I have a separate personal website where I challenge everyday situations that are taken for granted. The longest project I've worked on so far, Show Me Your Fridge, started ten years ago. This project started without any intention of earning money. Now I have photographed more than fifty fridges and their owners in cities including London, Paris, Berlin, Cape Town and Istanbul. With a light-hearted attitude, the viewer is invited to question their consumer behaviours. With this project I've had an exhibition at Horizonte Zingst, an environmental festival, and a group exhibition in Switzerland.

Recently, I teamed up with sustainable fashion consultant and advocate Julia Kline to document worn-out clothes. The project Show Me Your Closet aims to show how volatile our clothes are. We would like to create more awareness among consumers to treat their garments well in order to prolong their life. We advocate for a smart application of circularity in the fashion industry, envisioning a future where our old clothes could be reborn as a mushroom.

Show Me Your Fridge

You can't count on money to encourage you to get up in the morning

<u>Advice on gusto from FREAKS freearchitects</u>
<u>(Guillaume Aubry, Cyril Gauthier and Yves Pasquet)</u>

After some years of working abroad in different architecture practices, one day the three of us decided to launch our own practice. This did not correspond to winning a commission for a building, but to winning an award from the French Ministry of Culture (AJAP Prize). We want to underline that we did not start by working on a building project – as is usually the case – but rather by starting to look for projects. This is exactly when you have to add some gusto to the recipe; without enthusiasm and self-motivation, you can't count on either money or good feedback to encourage you to get up in the morning. Launching a business from scratch takes both courage and faith.

It might sound romantic to consider gusto as being the one and only ingredient required to run a practice and be successful, but there are lots of architects in the world. The good thing is that we are mostly quite good at what we do, the bad is that we are all so inspired by the ever-increasing amount of lookalike architecture images we see on the internet that we produce a more and more homogenous style of architecture. We FREAKS don't believe in revolutionizing architecture, we just want to achieve our projects by being sincere, smart, and efficient. Once the project is built, the second part of our story starts: documenting and promoting the project. That is when we really pull out all the stops. We could just take a nice set of pictures and send them to some blogs and magazines. No risk. So why do we go the extra mile? To prove to the rest of the world that we are in the game? To prove to ourselves that we are in the game? The answer is more selfish; it is much more fun to write a new scenario for each photoshoot, even more so when we perform ourselves

to activate the space/building. Distorting and questioning what a good architecture picture should be gives us so much pleasure that we consider it part of our job.

Whatever the scale is, whatever the fee is, what counts is being able to pick the projects that you really want to work on. We are very lucky to work in a field in which our job blends seamlessly with our pleasure and leisure. But don't forget to protect your own private life. What is the point of designing a restaurant, a bar, a cinema, if you do not have a minute of free time in your weekly routine to go out and experience it for real?

The last pandemic years we went through collectively have engaged everyone in re-balancing work and private life. Working remotely has definitely become a widely shared dynamic with which we all found both good qualities and faults, but it surely helped us all to realize that working is no longer just about being seated in the office. That is maybe the best conclusion and also the best advice to give to a young designer: get yourself a laptop so you can work from anywhere!

Credits

The author and publisher would like to thank the following institutions and individuals who provided images for use in this book. In all cases, every effort has been made to credit the copyright holders, but should there be any omissions or errors the publisher would be pleased to insert the appropriate acknowledgment in subsequent editions of this book.

14, 16 (t) Catherine Unger; **16 (b), 17** © SFB Games Ltd; **19** © Broken Rules
20, 23 Photos Skyler Fike, followskyfi.com; **22** Elisa Fisher Photography
24, 26, 27 Artwork and photos Jasmine MacPhee
28 Portrait of Alec Dudson by Sophie Lee
33 Sarah and Desmond, ICA Directors;
34 (t) Community Engagement; **34 (b)** Denny Art Strategy; **35** Social Enterprise Support Programme
37, 38 Photos Jody Hartley; **39 (t)** photo Anthony Mooney; **39 (b)** photo Jak Howard
40, 42, 43 © 2013 Justin Evidon www.justinevidon.com
44 Photo courtesy of Interface
48, 50, 51 Photos courtesy of Sound Advice
53, 54, 55 Stacie Woolsey, MYOM Alumni 2021, Makeversity
56 Photo Moise Luzolo; **58** Estelle at the eeH booth, Seek fashion trade show, Berlin, 2022, photo by Laurie Alaoua; **59** photo @raygun143
60 Photo © Sara Vaughan
64 Work in collaboration with Mateo Pinto and Carolina Cisneros, presented by Hester Street Collaborative; **66** work by the New York City Department of Transport; **67** work by the Architectural League of New York and Pen World Voices; **68 (b)** photo Tania Centenaro; **68 (t), 69** photos Stereotank
70, 72, 73 (t) Fabrice Le Nezet; **73 (b), 74, 75** Fabrice Le Nezet @ Optical Arts
76, 79, 80 (b) Jocelyn Ibarra; **78** Denis Rivin; **80 (t)** Mida Fiore; **81** Clara Llongarriu
82, 85 (b) Adam Nathaniel Furman, photography by Gareth Gardner; **84, 85 (t)** and **(m)** Adam Nathaniel Furman; **86 (t)** image courtesy Nuoveforme; **86 (b)** image © John Sturrock; **87** Adam Nathaniel Furman, image courtesy Botteganove

88, 90, 91 © VIN + OMI
92 © Cruz Garcia & Nathalie Frankowski of WAI Architecture Think Tank and Garcia Frankowski
97, 98, 99 © Noem9 Studio Ltd. All rights reserved www.noem9studio.com. All brand logos are the property of their legal authors.
100, 103 Photos Desia Ava; **102 (t)** photo Korina Kordova; **102 (b)** photo Danilo Donzelli
104 Photo by Jonathan Duval; **106** photo by LaPiscine; **107** photos by Marie-Michèle Larivée
108 Jimenez Lai, Bureau Spectacular
112 Photo courtesy of Branson Aquarium;
114 (t) photo by Studio Periphery; **114 (b)** installation collaboration with Reza Hasni, model: Joojin Lee, photo Irving Neil Kwok; **115 (t)** installation collaboration with Reza Hasni; **115 (b)** photo Space Objekt; **117** photos Chris Greenwell
119, 120, 121, 122 All work © State of Play Games Ltd.
124 Costume design: Ursula Kudma; **126 (b)** costume design: Nina Wetzel; **127 (t)** costume design: Katrin Wolfermann; all photos courtesy Werkstattkollektiv
128, 130, 131 Assemble Studio CIC
132, 134, 135 © The Glue Society; **136 (t)** The Glue Society/HBO; **136 (b)** conceived, written and directed by the Glue Society, produced by Revolver/Will O'Rourke
138 Photo by Piers Allardyce
143 'All you need and more' created for Lezilus;
144 (bl) 'City Tour' for Men's Health Germany;
144 (br) 'Mix' for Complex magazine
147, 148 (b) Obed Danjoint, Danjointphotography;
148 (t) Tristan Keith, Bubble Photography Studios;
149 Samuel Clark, ClarkFoto
151, 152, 153, 155 Studio SeeYa
156 © FREAKS

Author's acknowledgements

This book has been a huge part of my life. The completion of this new edition marks a new phase of my life also; so I dedicate this book to my daughter, Ren, and thank my partner Sarah for her endless support, in life and work.

I must also thank all of the friendly advisors who have provided encouragement and suggestions during the research period – you know who you are – and, of course, the myriad of incredible contributors who have dedicated their time and faith to the project.

Thank you.